Trees of India

Trees of India

Text by Dr. Subhadra Menon
Photography by Pallava Bagla

Local  Colour

Copyright © 2000 Local Colour Limited, Hong Kong
ppro@netvigator.com

Text copyright © 2000 Dr. Subhadra Menon
Photography copyright © 2000 Pallava Bagla

A CIP catalogue record for this is available from the British Library

Distributed in the United Kingdom and Europe by Hi Marketing
38 Carver Road, London SE24 9LT.
Fax: (0171) 274-9160

Distributed in the United States by Seven Hills Book Distributors
Fax: (888) 777-7799

ISBN 962-8711-12-1

9 8 7 6 5 4 3 2 1

Editor: Aruna Ghose

Design: Philip Choi

Printed and bound in China

CONTENTS

INTRODUCTION

*Which was the wood,
which the tree from which
they (the gods) shaped
heaven and earth?*

— Rig Veda

In many ancient cultures, trees are held sacred. It is as though sanctity stems from their ever-renewing force of life and growth. But nowhere else in the world do trees receive the veneration and love as accorded to them in India.

The Indian region's reverence for trees goes back to prehistory, to the animist beliefs of primitive peoples. Later it is evident in the seals of Mohenjo-Daro and Harappa, one of which depicts a horned goddess in a peepal tree. In other seals, woman and trees merge, seemingly in a common assertion of their fertility. Over the millennia tree-worship has continued unabated in countless shrines and sacred groves across the length and breadth of the region.

Like the forest canopy, a vast body of mythological and religious lore overspreads trees in India. Some were so greatly esteemed that they were believed to personify no less than the Supreme Being. Shiva himself is *sthanu* or a tree trunk devoid of leaves, and the ber is sacred to him. Vishnu is said to manifest himself in the peepal, which of course is also the tree under which Buddha attained enlightenment and the tongues of bells in Buddhist temples in Myanmar are shaped like peepal leaves.

Other trees are associated with specific gods. Thus Krishna recalls the kadamba, under whose boughs he played his flute and into whose branches he escaped after stealing the *gopis'* clothes. He is also associated with the night-fragrant harsingar or paarijat, which he is said to have stolen from the garden of Indra, the king of the gods. The mango tree is the abode of Kama, god of love, and his cupid arrows are tipped with mango blossoms. The banyan is the tree of Savitri, who reclaimed her husband from death, and is hence the patron deity of good Hindu wives. Nepalese folk believe the semal to be the abode of evil spirits, and that sinners in hell are tortured with its large thorns.

All these are part of the country's rich botanical inheritance but ancient India went further to invent the mythical kalpavriksha, the wish-fulfilling tree at whose roots lay pots of gold and bags of jewels. There are no records of this tree having actually existed. There is the mythical Speaking Tree, gifted with oracular powers, believed to have warned Alexander the Great that he would never conquer India. Called the Waqwaq Tree in Islamic tradition, it is painted in Mughal miniatures with a trunk

In western India *Alstonia scholaris*, which is also called shaitan, or Devil's Tree, is believed to be the abode of evil spirits

(facing page) Coniferous pine forest and snow in the Himalayas in Garhwal, Uttar Pradesh

7

(above and below) Trees frequently appear as motifs on cloth in different styles across India

(right) An old ber tree is garlanded and worshipped at the Golden Temple in Amritsar, Punjab

Trees frequently appear as motifs on cloth in different styles across India

formed of snakes, and sprouting animal heads and beautiful women from its boughs.

Inhabiting trees, both real and imagined, were a host of sylvan creatures, nature spirits considered worthy of worship. One such was the yakshi, a tree nymph who sometimes appeared as a salabhanjika, bearer of flowers from the majestic sal tree so common in the region. The apsaras or celestial damsels dwelled in trees and bore the names of sweet-scented herbs and flowers. Arising in the fertility cults of remote antiquity, the connection between trees and the sacred female was absorbed into Hinduism. Trees sheltered female deities and contained their essence and divinity. The Atharva Veda equates plants with the Mother Goddess, and the Bhavishya Purana enjoins worship of Durga as present in the bel tree.

Given this religious and cultural ethos, common beliefs surrounding trees are legion. The ashoka dispels sorrow, the neem bestows happiness, the mandar gladdens the sun. Women unable to conceive must pray to the peepal to be blessed with offspring. It is also of special importance to Brahmin children before their thread ceremony, when they are initiated into the rigours and faiths of their religion. In south India, most peepal trees are surrounded by a concrete platform on which are placed three naga or snake stones and offerings of

prasad are smeared on its trunk. The amla is also sacred, as is the kikar, sometimes seen dense with clay pots tied to its branches to placate the gods. In the Himalayas, the deodar, "tree of the gods", is worshipped and grown in the vicinity of hill temples. Through much of the south, it is the coconut tree that symbolises prosperity. An entire Nair wedding takes place around a flowering coconut twig embedded in a vessel full of rice grain. In most Muslim homes of the region each day's fast during the month of Ramadan is normally broken by eating a date palm. Buddhist monks in Myanmar and Thailand wear robes coloured with a yellow dye produced from the jackfruit's wood.

The regard and reverence given to individual trees is matched by the sanctity of groves and forest glades, thought to be the best possible environment for cultivating concentration, memory and philosophic speculation. In India, abodes too have been deified. Even today the archaic Indian idyll of the forest retreat has a profound emotional appeal. This is recalled in the myth of Uttarakuru, the Hindu paradise. The Kurus, protagonists of the Mahabharata along with the Pandavas, enjoyed a legendary reputation — they inhabited a land never brought under the plough, a place of the gods, a kind of Olympus, and Buddhist texts speak of it as "the Golden Land where there

Thanjavur painting depicting Krishna playing the flute

Zizyphus mauritiana is revered by Sikhs

is absolute calm and its trees bear no thorns".

Recorded history abounds in references to trees. School children remember Emperor Ashoka for having planted shade trees along highways to shelter sun-scorched travellers. Other kings followed his example. The Greek Megasthenes describes with awe the splendid parks surrounding the palace of Chandragupta Maurya. The seventh century Chinese traveller Hsuan Tsang's account states that dense jungle lined the Ganga for miles on end. There is even a southern ruling dynasty, the Kadambas, named after the tree, because legend has it that the first of them sprang up under the kadamba tree out of a drop of sweat from Shiva's brow.

With the advent of Islam there arose the concept of the formal garden, an analogue of the Gardens of Paradise. Its char-bagh or four-quartered plan had precise instructions for the placement of water channels, flowering shrubs and trees. The first Mughal emperor Babur, enchanted by the gardens of Samarkand and Herat, responded to the heat and dust of India by laying out gardens. His memoirs, the Babur-Nama, has one whole section devoted to the trees and fruits of Hindustan. He was emulated by successive Mughal rulers, notably Jahangir and Shah Jahan. While the accent in the early Mughal gardens was on shrubs and flowers, trees figured prominently in the later gardens — the

The tree as represented in a colourful Madhubani tribal painting

A Mughal miniature painting of a banyan tree sheltering a Sufi saint

Yakshi, eastern gateway, Stupa No.1, 2nd century BC, Sanchi, Madhya Pradesh

chinar (in Kashmir), the aspen, the cypress; and fruit trees including the apple, quince and plum.

The tree has always been an important motif in art. C. Sivaramamurti in *The Art of India* cites several sculptural examples — a graphic wish-fulfilling tree spilling forth treasures from Nachna, Madhya Pradesh; Buddhist panels from Bharhut showing an ancient tradition of tree-worship; a *salabhanjika* adorning the torana or gateway at Sanchi Madhya Pradesh; and a Gupta sculpture from Deogarh with Vishnu as Narayana under the badari or ber tree. One of the sights of Ahmedabad is a pierced window screen of a mosque with the delicate tracery of a palm and creeper motif in sandstone filigree.

Although trees were represented in paintings from the earliest times, perhaps their fullest flowering came with the miniature schools, where meticulous care and love appears to have been lavished on each trunk and branch, flower and leaf. The early Mughal miniatures inspired by the Persians had a predilection for the straight-trunked cypress and plane. But as Mughal art became more independent, the painters set down the great trees of the Indian plains, revelling in their green luxuriance. Some schools can be distinguished by the way in which trees were depicted. To take just one example, the Basohli painters reveal an amazing inventiveness in the stylization of trees such as

the pomegranate, flame of the forest, mango and horse-chestnut. Love-sick heroines languish under the drooping willow; spire-like trees protectively surround the trysts of lovers; and a forest is often indicated by a circle of trees.

In the art of tribal people, living in close consonance with nature, trees assume a delightfully fresh and naive aspect. This is true of colour-drenched Madhubani art, but it is especially so of Warli paintings where fragile foliage is etched in white against a rich earth-coloured ground. Writing of these in *The Earthen Drum,* Pupul Jayakar says: "The images could have been born of the Atharva Veda hymns, of the glory of virgin forests and the sacral spirit of tree divinities... There was in the paintings a primeval tree, knowing each tree was alive, creating a luminous light-filled world of splendid trees, hundred-branched with outstretched leaves, 'fortunate, God-quickened, powerful'."

The line between art and craft is drawn on water, impermanent and illusory. Here too, in the many-faceted world of crafts, trees manifest themselves in countless ways — under the wood carver's chisel, through the magic of the weaver's loom and the printer's block, and in the smelter of the metal worker.

Along with art and craft, literature too mirrors a culture, and there are innumerable Indian literary references to trees. Long passages

Offerings of prasad smeared on a peepal tree

Prayers and offerings being bestowed upon an amla tree, *Emblica officinalis*

The Tamarind tree on the tomb of the famous singer Tansen in Gwalior. Singers eat the leaves of this imli tree to render their voices as sweet as Tansen's

Worship of Bodhi Tree, pillar from the Bharhut Stupa, 2nd century BC, Indian Museum, Calcutta

Bamboo yard in Madhya Pradesh

Tree motifs in Madhubani tribal paintings

A Ganesha carving made from sandalwood

11

in the Mahabharata and Ramayana describe the kalpavriksha. The Buddhist Jataka tales tell of similar trees inhabited by deities who feed and clothe weary travellers. Kalidasa in Shakuntala refers to kindly forest spirits who cared for the simple hermit girl. Perhaps more than any other work of literature the Gita Govinda, a poem that sings of the love of Radha and Krishna, is redolent of the forest, set as it is amidst bowers and arbours. A verse from the poet Vidyapati's version says:

"In our two hearts
Those shoots of love
Opened with two or three leaves.
Then grew the branches
And the clusters of foliage.
They were covered with flowers
And scent lay everywhere."

(above) The lush, ever-green maulshree, *Minusops elengi*

(left above) A jamun tree, *Syzygium cumini*, best loved across the subcontinent for its deep purple berries

(facing page) An 'Ashok' tree, *Polyalthia longifolia*

(left below) Lush forests of sal trees in Uttar Pradesh, northern India

(below) A silk cotton tree with knotted branches

(right) Flowers of the amaltas, *Cassia fistula*

(far right) Flowers of the *Callistemon lanceolatus*

(right) *Erythrian suberosa* tree in full bloom

(far right) *Rhododendron* flowers

The forests and trees become a symbol of the yearning of lovers. The poet compares red palash flowers, curved like the crescent moon, to nail marks imprinted by a lover. Weddings are arranged between trees — in south India the peepal and neem are grown close together and a ceremonial marriage is solemnised between the two. There are also matings of trees and creepers — for example, the mango tree and the bauhinia liana. In Nepal, young girls are often married to a bel tree, in the belief that upon their husband's later death they will not become a widow.

Indeed trees are often imbued with human feelings, they are seen as sentient beings with the ability to experience joy and pain. Stella Kramrisch in *The Hindu Temple* tells of how the axe to cut the sacrificial post is invoked. "O axe, hurt it not", and prior to the fatal blow a blade of darbha grass is laid on the tree with the words, "O herb, protect it." Later an offering is made above the cut surface praying that the tree may grow again with a hundred branches. Trees could grieve, as when they scattered flowers like teardrops at the reluctant abandonment of Sita by Rama. The ability of trees to respond to human love gave rise to the concept of dohada, the power of a young girl to make a plant bloom out of its normal season — the kuruvaka puts forth blossoms when embraced by a damsel and the bakula when sprinkled with mouthfuls of wine. Less demanding is the kesara, moved merely by a maiden's loving glances.

All in all, the Indian association with trees is a dense matrix, as many-stranded and interwoven as the roots of the banyan. It is an acknowledgement that man and tree are closely connected in their life and fate, an aspect of the wider interdependence of man and nature. Yet, somewhere in this complex coexistence, humans have turned exploiters, The 20th century has seen a grave annihilation of these very trees and forests, a plunder so terrible that vast tracts of precious forests have disappeared over the years. Tree cover in the Indian subcontinent has declined drastically during the last century. It might be time to rekindle some of the religious, emotional and reverential bonds that India has very clearly witnessed in the past. A time for man and trees to become friends once more. This would be the ultimate manifestation of the human belief in the essential unity of all living things.

(top) *Holoptelia integrifolia*

(above) Trees across the subcontinent have been shorn clean of leaves for cattle fodder

(left) A fossilised leaf of *Salix wallichiana*, (a living species) from the Fossil National Park in Madhya Pradesh

Clouds forming over rain-forests in Arunachal
Pradesh

Cherry like bright red fruit of *ficus mysorensis,* a relative of the bargad from the fig family

(following spread) The flowers of the Gulmohur tree

Pine or *Pinus roxburghii* tree

(facing page) Neem or Azadhirachta indica tree

(above top) A timber yard in a plywood factory at Tinsukia in northeast India

(above middle) A tribal walks through a lush teak forest which is going to be axed as it falls within the submergence zone of the Narmarda Sagar Dam on the Narmarda River in central India

(above) A stack of fuel wood near Lucknow in northern India

(left) A giant Arjun tree being felled by six wood-cutters. This tree was being cut down as it was within the submergence zone of the Narmarda Sagar Dam

Amaltas or *Cassia fistula* tree

(facing page) Forests in the Great Himalayan National Park, Himachal Pradesh

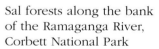

A lone majestic tree silhouetted against the evening sun. Kaziranga National Park in Assam

Sal forests along the bank of the Ramaganga River, Corbett National Park

27

A lovely silk cotton tree at sunset

(facing page) Tall, clean bole of *Boswelia* – salai – tree

ABOUT THIS BOOK

The Indian subcontinent has an incredible diversity of plant life. There are 15,000 known species of flowering plants alone, of which around 2,500 are trees. This book gives an in-depth portrait of 60 of the best known, most beautiful and useful trees. Limiting the number to 60 has been extremely difficult and, despite the care and thought accompanying the selection, it might well be that some important trees have been left out. This is regrettable but, sadly, unavoidable.

Trees of the Indian Subcontinent has a dual purpose — to provide comprehensive informa-tion about each plant as well as to help the tree-lover to recognise each species by identifying its particular characteristics that make it unique. While there are many books on Indian trees, few have laid equal stress on high quality pictures and accurate text. This is one such attempt.

Here, each tree is provided with its common Hindi and English names, in addition to the scientific Latin name and their botanical family. The Latin term is actually two words — the first denotes the genus and the second is what is called a specific epithet, indicating the particular plant species. The vernacular name usually has

Slash and burn cultivation has denuded hillsides such as this one in Mizoram, eastern India

(facing page):

(above) Burnt trees at the Silent Valley National Park in southern India.

(middle) Forests around the country, including the pristine rainforests of the Andaman Islands, have been encroached upon by civilisation

(below) Arunachal Pradesh in eastern India has one of the few closed canopy, lush rainforests in the Indian subcontinent

regional equivalents in the various different local languages. These, however, are not mentioned here. The trees featured are grouped according to their botanical family. At the end of the main descriptive text there are brief sections covering non-flowering trees, palms, fruits and bamboos. However, some important trees from these groups also appear in the main text.

The trees of the Indian subcontinent are generally divided into six major groups. These are moist tropical forests, dry tropical forests, montane subtropical forests, montane temperate forests, subalpine forests and alpine scrub. Each of these has a large number of sub-groups, which fall beyond the scope of this note. While most of the 60 trees in this book are flowering plants or angiosperms, some belong to the conifer group, known as gymnosperms, which are non-flowering and mainly to be found in the Himalayan region. Any book on trees would be incomplete without these lofty and majestic specimens, the source of much forest produce.

A vast number of mythological and religious beliefs are associated with trees of this region (see Introduction). This aspect apart, trees are vital for human life — as shade-givers, havens for animals and birds, soil-binding, and to control the climate in the form of forests. The value of Indian forests in water regulation and flood control is estimated at a huge US$72 billion. Yet, it is this very value and utility that have made forests vulnerable to human plunder.

Deforestation and degradation of the land all over the world has increased enormously over the last 40 years. India is thirteenth on the United Nations – Food and Agriculture Organisation's listing of the top 20 nations in the production of industrial roundwood (in technical forestry language, roundwood is a term for all wood products, excluding fuel and charcoal). This constitutes 25 million cubic metres, two per cent of the total world production. More importantly, there is a gene pool of wild trees and native species of the region that is constantly being misused and denuded, because of a weak system of intellectual property rights. Today gene pirates work relentlessly through enormous banks of germ-plasm; the chainsaws fell the giant trees of the rainforests; and land developers clear vast tracts of precious forests for housing and factories.

It is imperative that these trends be halted by conscious human action and intervention. Our natural heritage is too precious to be so wantonly destroyed for our immediate needs. Perhaps this book will go a little way towards achieving this – in preserving, for future generations, the priceless green gold of the Indian subcontinent.

Mango Tree, *Aam*

Mangifera indica, Family Anacardiaceae

Claims regarding the antiquity of the domesticated mango tree range between 2000 and 4000 years. It is said to have been found by Alexander the Great's army when it entered the Indus Valley in 327 B.C. The stupa at Sanchi, dated 150 B.C., carries representations of the mango tree. In Hindu mythology, it is immortalised as a wish-fulfilling tree. It is believed to be an incarnation of Prajapati, lord of all creatures, and the abode of Kama, the God of love. Mango flowers are dedicated to the moon. To Buddhists, it is a sacred tree.

So auspicious is the mango tree that strings of its leaves festoon marriage halls; leaf garlands adorn a house entrance when a son is born; and its wood is used for the havan or fire sacrifice and in funeral pyres. The mango tree grows wild in India, Myanmar and Sri Lanka.

All this is apart from the fact that the mango is by far the best-loved fruit in this part of the world. With its universal appeal, the mango is widely cultivated in many different varieties, such as alphonso, langra, dashehri, amrapalli and malgoa each singular in its flavour.

Evergreen and with an impressive canopy, the mango tree is large, growing to heights of 20-25 metres. This upright, well-branched tree has a dense, rounded canopy sometimes stretched to a column-like shape. The trunk is covered with a rough thick brown bark which is lightly fissured. The branches may rise from one point giving shape to a round canopy, but there are trees where the main trunk remains undivided and individual branches grow out somewhat haphazardly from different points in the tree. In fact, the tree is well-known as a shade-

(left) Bunches of pale mango flowers smother the tree when it is in full bloom, (facing page) Full Mango tree *Mangifera indica*

33

A mango motif made from cloth

Unripe and ripe fruit of the mango tree

(below) Several varieties of mangoes find their way into markets both in India and overseas

(below right) Mango motifs such as this one displayed at the Mango Festival, New Delhi, find expression in art throughout the region

giver. Mango leaves are simple, elongated, dark green and glossy. Each leaf has wavy margins and a pointed tip, and is slightly thick and brittle. They are fragrant when crushed and smelt.

Depending on the variety, the mango tree flowers between January and April. Heavy and lush open bunches of flowers or panicles totally cover the tree, which takes on a reddish hue, since the flowers are pale yellow or reddish with hues of green. These minute flowers are almost countless, and male or bisexual flowers are all borne together on the same bunch. The single flower has petals twice the length of its sepals.

The arrival of the mango season between

April and July is a much-celebrated event. The fleshy golden yellow drupe is ovoid and somewhat flattened at both ends. Only the fruit wall portion that is fleshy — called the mesocarp — is eaten. The seed within is large, hard and non-edible, covered with numerous fibres. The fruit of different varieties are all distinctive in taste.

Though best known for its fruit, the mango tree has a large number of other practical uses. The wood, despite its inferior quality, is used to make window-frames, packing cases, farm implements and shoe-heels. The bark and seeds are medicinally valuable, against heamorrhage and asthma respectively.

Mast Tree, *Ashok*

Polyalthia longifolia, Family Annonaceae

Often confused with *Saraca indica*, which has the same common Indian name, the mast tree or "false ashoka" resembles a pole with foliage. Actually, the two trees are totally dissimilar — the former has coral red blossoms while this one has the most insignificant flowers. This is an extremely common tree, its elegant form growing ubiquitously along avenues and it is popular for its lengthy form. This lofty tree can be found all over India and Sri Lanka.

The tree has a straight trunk covered with a smooth, greyish-brown bark. The branches that emerge from the cylindrical column grow in a peculiar down-sweeping manner, which constitutes its most characteristic feature.

The leaves of this tree are glossy and dark

Tall, straight and elegant false ashoka trees are commonly found across the subcontinent

green, typically long and lancet-like in shape.
With wavy margins and pointed tips, they
resemble mango leaves. Each leaf is around 15-
20 cms long. Being an evergreen tree, the ashok
never sheds its leaves, appearing most attractive
when the reddish new foliage and the old leaves
are found together. The leaves are often used in
place of mango leaves to adorn doorways and
gateways during Hindu festivals and ceremonies.

This tree has inconspicous flowers — very
small and whitish-green in colour. It flowers from
February through April. Clusters of these star-
shaped flowers look like tiny umbrellas, which is
why they are called umbels. The individual
flower is borne on a small stalk and has small
sepals that surround the six lance-shaped petals.

This ashok gets covered with fruit during
the summer. Borne on short stalks, the ovoid
fruits, black when ripe, are an important source
of food for many animals, especially bats.

The popular style of manicured gardening
and landscaping finds a great tool in this tree. It
is the first to be planted in new residential areas
and homes, because they soon become a tall
green wall. Yet, it is not a tree that can withstand
too much wind, and often requires sheltered
planting. Other than its decorative use, the wood
is used to make barrels and drums, and as a
scaffolding material.

Devil's Tree, *Shaitan*

Alstonia scholaris, Family Apocynaceae

In western India, this tree is believed to be the abode of evil spirits, hence its name. Usually a small to medium-sized tree, the shaitan reaches a maximum height of 14-15 metres. It has very distinctive foliage, dark green leaves that look like the palm of a human hand and are clustered together. The rich, glossy leaves and the heady-smelling flowers make this evergreen a popular ornamental tree. The somewhat column-like but rounded crown of the branches often look like an inverted cone, and a dense one or that.

The rough bark of the shaitan is dark grey on the outer side and yellowish inside. Since several branches emerge at the same height on the main trunk, they have a whorled or some-what spiral appearance. The shaitan is commonly seen all along the sub-Himalayan region, and grows well throughout India, Myanmar, Sri Lanka, and the Malay Archipelago.

The simple, leathery leaves are oblong and dark green on the upper surface. The lower surface is whitish. One single whorl has four to seven leaves and each leaf is entire with acute tips. The leaves exude a milky secretion and are parallel-veined.

The very sweet-smelling flowers, small and greenish-white, are grouped into small clusters and arranged in compact units that droop slightly. These units are so formed that the main, central axis of the inflorescence has one single flower that develops first. The other secondary branches of the inflorescence flower later and the whole unit that emerges from the centre of a leaf-whorl is called a cyme. Each flower has five sepals and the petals are fused into the shape of a tube called the corolla tube. The flowers appear from September to November.

The fruit is a dry vessel containing one seed. It is very narrow and somewhat sickle-shaped. With pointed, tapering ends, these follicles break open from a suture on their lower surface to release the seed. The fruits appear between March and June hanging down in bunches.

'Ditta bark', a commercial name for the shaitan's medicinally valuable bark, is very useful against worm infections, besides being a good astringent. It is useful also because it has a wide array of alkaloids. The shaitan's wood is rather soft, making it useful for building temporary structures and packing-cases. The scholaris in the plant's botanical name apparently comes from its past use as a timber source for blackboards.

Alstonia scholaris is a popular ornamental tree

(right) *Alstonia scholaris* has very distinctive leaves that look like the palm of a human hand and are clustered together

(below) Detail of the bark of the *Alstonia scholaris* tree (below right) the sweet smelling flowers can be seen from September to November

Yellow Oleander, *Peela Kaner*

Thevetia peruviana, Family Apocynaceae

More like a shrub, with very attractive yellow, bell-shaped flowers, this tree grows to about 5-8 metres. Its glossy dark green leaves are like slender lances. The main trunk and branches grow and spread in a regular fashion and the trunk is covered with a thin, smooth greyish-brown bark.

The peela kaner is evergreen and the leaves are arranged in a manner that makes the tree easy to recognise — alternate to each other, they emerge in a spiral of glossy twists and turns.

The most notable aspect of this tree is its flowers, which remain on the tree for the greater part of the year. They are large, yellow and fragrant. The five overlapping petals form a bell-shaped structure and the sepals are distinct and bright green. These flowers are borne in clusters that have two or three blossoms each.

The round and distinctly bi-partitioned fruit has a stone which in turn consists of the seeds. It is technically called a drupe. It forms a triangular bag that is hard when ripe.

The peela kaner has significant medicinal properties. Of great therapeutic value in the plant is peruvoside, a cardiac glycoside. The leaves are good purgatives and the root-paste is a cure for tumours.

The most notable aspect of the peela kaner is its flowers, which remain on the tree for a greater part of the year. The flowers are large, yellow and fragrant

Frangipani, *Safed Champa*

Plumeria alba, Family Apocynaceae

The *Plumeria alba* tree is a sacred tree for Hindus, Muslims and Buddhists

Plumeria alba flowers can sometimes bloom even after the tree has been uprooted

The ability of the frangipani to bloom even after it has been uprooted has made it a symbol of immortality. This is why Muslims and Buddhists plant it near their tombs. For Hindus too, the tree is sacred and its flowers are offered to deities. This small and rather delicate tree with its gorgeous, fragrant flowers is neither large nor too impressive, growing to a maximum height of 6-8 metres. The beauty of the frangipani lies in its artistic branching pattern, large and generous leaves and flowers. The tree grows all over India, Myanmar and the Malay Archipelago.

Like all plants of this family, the frangipani has an abundance of milky latex. The main trunk is very rarely distinguishable from its primary branches because they begin very low from the ground and the trunk is not much thicker. The bark is smooth and whitish-grey. The main trunk is short, has distinct knots, and is quite crooked. The canopy is round and flattened on the top, with the main branches tending to taper slightly towards their ends. Young branches are shiny and succulent.

The leaves are large, oblong and thick, green but with silky hairs that give them a whitish appearance. The veins are very prominent, running parallel till the edge of the leaf. The leaves are borne in bunches, where they are spirally arranged, with juicy stalks at least 5-8 cms long. The leaves are also full of latex. In its natural habitat the tree is deciduous and has no leaves right through the hot season.

The frangipani flowers all year round. Each flower is silky and creamy-white, with five petals. The flowers, in clusters called cymes, are highly fragrant and have a petal tube in which the filaments of the anthers are hidden. Above this tube the petals are broad and oval, with one margin each curling inwards. The flowers are suffused with yellow at the base. *Plumeria rubra* is another species which has bright pink flowers. Even after they fall to the ground, these flowers remain fresh and sweet-smelling. The fruit is a long pod but is never seen.

The frangipani is planted mainly for its beauty. Its glamorous, deeply scented flowers are popular omanents. The bark and latex both have several medicinal properties and the termite-resistant wood is used to make musical instruments.

Coconut, *Nariyal*

Cocos nucifera, Family Arecaceae

(left) Groves of coconut trees can be seen all over peninsular India

(far left) A rare branched coconut from the Nicobar Islands in the Bay of Bengal.

Few trees in India are considered as auspicious as the coconut, an essential part of numerous religious and social observances. In Gujarat, it is treated as a family god and in parts of the Deccan, Muslims throw bits of coconut and lime over the bridegroom's head to avert evil spirits. The tall, slender trunk of this palm reaching 20-30 metres in height does not increase in girth with maturity, giving the tree its gracefully slim appearance. Ringed prominently with left-over scars of old leaves, the coconut trunk is often rather deeply curved, which makes for the tree's picturesque profile. The coconut is found growing profusely all over peninsular India, especially along the two coasts and the northeast, as well as in Myanmar, Sri Lanka and the Malay Archipelago.

The trunk, which is very rarely branched, is thickened at the base with a clump of rootlets, and this swollen base is often inclined to one side. The more or less uniform diameter of the trunk all through its considerable length is about 40-70 cms and the soft nature of the coconut's wood causes the main trunk to bend. Along the backwaters of India's southern coastal states, deeply curved trees arched over the water make a striking sight, an attractive perch for children.

The leaves of this tree, as with all palms, are like huge, feathery brooms. Reaching a length of 2-4 metres, each leaf has a strong, thick central axis which has long and linear leaflets on both sides with pointed tips and stout stalks or petioles. Almost 100 leaflets can form a leaf. All the leaves, bright and glossy green, are bunched at the summit to form the typical palm leaf crown.

Coconut flowers are as distinctive and as special as the rest of the tree. Male and female flowers, although separate, are borne on the same tree. Numerous, drooping branchlets bear the small collection of two or three ovoid female flowers at the base, and the upper portion is densely covered with lots of small male flowers. Female flowers are larger. The coconut inflorescence is a hardy spadix and is called androgynous because it has both male and female flowers. The whole floral spray is enclosed in a sheath, and the flowers are a creamy-white.

The fruit is the famous coconut, large and roughly oval, often likened in shape to a human head. It is botanically called a drupe, the term for describing a fruit that has an outer skin, a pulpy inner layer or mesocarp and a single seed within. In the mature coconut there is a fibrous outer layer and then a hard shell which is closely adhered by a white fleshy layer. The coconut milk or water that is drunk is the nourishing tissue of the fruit called the endosperm. The whole fruit is about 20-30 cms long and its hard shell has three pores that represent the three cells of the ovary. The fruit needs almost ten months to mature, and coconut trees flower all the year round, though it takes several years before it begins to flower.

The multiple uses of the coconut tree have perhaps meant more to human civilisation than any other single tree. Some call it "green gold". It is a true symbol of prosperity and generosity because the belief is that it takes up the ordinary water of the earth, sweetens it and returns it to human beings. From the wood that is used for construction purposes, the leaves for weaving and thatching, the fruit for a multitude of reasons and the fibre for making ropes, matting and brushes, the tree is a veritable treasure trove. Oil from the coconut is used worldwide, the milk is used in scientific research, particularly for culturing tissues, since it has a tremendous nutritive value. The coconut tree is sacred to millions of Indians, and a Nair wedding in Kerala can only be solemnised in front of a coconut floral spray embedded in a bowl of rice.

Water from the coconut is used in scientific research, paticularly for culturing tissues

A roadside coconut seller is a common sight in south India

Coconuts are used in religious ceremonies around the region

Jacaranda, *Jamuni Badal*

Jacaranda mimosifolia, Family Bignoniaceae

(previous spread) *Jacaranda mimosifolia* in bloom with its blue-mauve flowers

(below) *Jacaranda mimosifolia* flowers

(below right) The fragrant timber of the jacaranda is often called "false rosewood"

With its blue-mauve clouds of flowers, the jacaranda is a tree of exceptionally delicate beauty. Indeed, it is difficult to understand why this native of Brazil is not more widely planted. The jacaranda is a small tree, reaching a maximum height of 12 metres, with slender branches and feathery foliage. The branches begin to emerge very high above the ground and their diversification is fairly symmetrical. The large number of smaller, fine branches towards the ends of the main branches give the tree canopy an irregular appearance. The trunk is covered with a dull greyish-black bark that is quite smooth.

The compound leaves, feathery in appearance and made up of 16-18 pairs of smaller units called pinnae, in turn bear 14-24 pairs of small light green leaflets. Each pinna is placed exactly opposite its pair on either side of the main leaf stalk. Each leaflet is pointed at the tip, and the top leaflet is always larger than the rest.

The mauve blossoms of the jacaranda are quite unparalleled in their loveliness. Drooping and slightly pyramidal in shape, each loose, branched floral cluster is filled with roughly 50 tube-like flowers. Each flower has a small set of sepals and a five-lobed tube of petals, of which three are bigger than the others. About two-thirds of the length of the petals is fused into the tube, and the tips of the clusters have buds. The fruit is a brown, oblong and a hard capsule that bursts open when ripe. The seeds are winged.

The fragrant timber of the jacaranda is often called "false rosewood". It is used to make furniture, cabinets and tool-handles. The bark and leaves have medicinal value. But its greatest value is its beauty.

Common Sausage Tree, *Kajelia*

Kigelia pinnata, Family Bignoniaceae

The unusual name of this native of Africa stems from the huge sausage-shaped fruit that hang down from its branches. A medium-sized tree that grows to about 12-15 metres, it has a dense and roughly round canopy. The trunk, covered in a coarse grey-brown bark, is stout and branches very close to the ground.

The leaves are compound and each has seven or nine pairs of simple oblong leaflets, smooth on the upper surface and slightly hairy underneath. These dark green leaflets that always cover this evergreen tree are about 10 cms in length and 8 cms in width. The leaflets are directly attached onto the main leaf stalk.

The sausage tree blooms between May and July. The flowers are the colour of red wine and are large and showy, formed into inflorescences. These heavy bunches hang downwards in pendulous fashion. Each flower,

distinct from a distance, is bell-shaped and has a tube-like group of petals, yellow at the base and red on top. These foul-smelling flowers, fleshy and velvety to the touch, open at night and are pollinated by bats.

Of the 30-40 flowers that make up one floral cluster barely one or two finally develop into the massive and typical fruit. The fruit, brownish-grey, woody and gourd-like, grow to 60-90 cms in length and hang down on rope-like stalks. They have a fibrous pulp embedded with many seeds, and are quite heavy.

The fruit of the common sausage tree has medicinal properties and although the pulp is not edible, it is effective as a sore-dressing for syphilis patients and the bark is often used to cure rheumatism and dysentery. It is also a popular ornamental tree because of the excellent shade it provides.

(top)*Kigelia pinnata* flower and (below left) leaves

Kigelia pinnata flowers grow in floral clusters of 30–40 flowers

Yellow Tabebuia, *Peela Tabebia*

Tabebuia argentea, Family Bignoniaceae

Tabebuia argentea is usually quite plain, but is covered with beautiful yellow flowers when it blooms

The flowers of *Tabebuia argentea* appear from April to June

Unusually plain and unadorned, this tree undergoes a transformation when it blooms — large, yellow funnel-like flowers appear in clusters at the ends of its branches. The tabebuia is generally a medium-sized tree, growing to a height of about 12-15 metres. The canopy is oval to round and branches grow in all directions. This deciduous tree is usually grown for its ornamental value.

The leaves are compound and are made up of three to five leaflets arranged in a human palm-like fashion. These leaflets are all subtended on slightly long and prominent petioles or stalks that radiate outwards from the centre of

the compound leaf. Each leaflet is oval or almost oblong and can be between 10-16 cms long and 6-8 cms broad, each clustering into a large leaf.

The flowers of this tree, appearing from April to June, are its most memorable feature. Although this is true of most trees, it is more obvious in those that have neither impressive canopies nor foliage, which is the case here. But when the flowering season begins, and the funnels of the large yellow flowers are massed on the branches, the tree presents a dramatic sight.

The fruit is seldom seen on the tree because most of the funnel-shaped flowers fall off before fruiting can take place. This prolific abscission of flowers, as it is technically called, is so great that there is always a carpet of flowers under the tree. The fruit, when it does form, is a capsule containing many winged seeds.

The yellow tabebuia is often planted in gardens and as an avenue tree. The bark and fruit have medicinal properties and are used as diuretics and antipyretics, in fact the peel of the fruit is also used as a hypnotising agent. The wood is called West Indian boxwood and is moderately useful as material for interior construction. This wood is utilised in furniture and cabinet work.

A yellow tabebuia tree in full bloom

Floss-silk Tree, *Resham Rui*

Chorisia speciosa, Family Bombacaceae

A *Chorisia speciosa* tree in bloom

A flamboyant, pink *Chorisia speciosa* flower

green spikes are well-matched with the green-white bark that covers the trunk. This bark is thick, smooth and waxy. With branches that grow horizontally and vertically, the floss-silk has an attractive canopy, somewhat cylindrical or like a column. If one finds a tree with a green trunk and conical prickles, one can be quite sure it is the floss-silk. The tree, when in full bloom, looks very pretty against the blue sky.

The leaves are compound, made up of five to seven leaflets that appear distinctly like the palm of a hand. These palmate leaflets are dark green and leathery to the touch and have pointed ends and slightly jagged margins. Leaf fall occurs in the winter months between December and February leaving the tree stark.

The floss-silk is grown primarily for its beautiful flowers. The elongated petals are fleshy and the stamens are fused into the shape of a tube. These large flowers fall on ageing and carpet the ground around the tree. The fruit is an oval pod with many seeds packed into a white silky cotton base.

The floss is used to fill cushions. The wood is soft, and is used for making match-sticks and pulp. The tree often is centre-piece in gardens.

The large, flamboyant pink flowers of the floss-silk tree are its major asset. A medium-sized tree growing to a maximum height of about 10-12 metres, the floss-silk is very easy to identify because of its thick and prominent spikes that cover the whole trunk like an armour. These

Silk Cotton Tree, *Semal*

Salmalia malabarica, Family Bombacaceae

Dominating the landscape wherever it grows, the semal is tall and robust, with an impressive crown and showy, scarlet flowers. The tree is from the same family as the floss-silk or Chorisia and the two are similar in their branching pattern, and foliage, which is very attractive. The semal is commonly seen all over the region — in India, Myanmar, Sri Lanka and the Malay Archipelago.

The semal easily grows to heights of 25-30 metres. The trunk is covered with stout prickly spines when the tree is young but is smooth at maturity. The trunk is often found with prominent buttresses supporting the large tree. The bark is smooth and greyish-brown. The main branches growing out of the trunk are horizontal, arranged around the main stem in whorls of two or three each, out of which palm-like leaves grow.

The semal has large compound leaves. They are shaped like the human hand and are therefore called palmately compound. Each such hand-like leaf has three to seven leaflets, about 10-12 cms in length and broadly oval in shape. They are dark green and slightly rough. The semal is deciduous, shedding its foliage between the months of December and February.

At its best when in bloom between February and April, the semal's flamboyant flowers are big, thick and grow in clusters of bright red.

Salmalia malabarica flowers are big, thick and red, and bloom in clusters between February and April

A bare Silk Cotton tree showing the thorns on the trunk

(facing page) The big red flowers are full of sweet rectar

A *bare Salmalia malabarica* tree

A *Salmalia malabarica* tree in bloom

SILK COTTON TREE
Bombax malabaricum, DC.
(¹/₂ nat. size)

Each flower has a thick, cup-shaped silky calyx. The petals are five, glossy, rather fleshy and delicately veined. The stamens that bear the anthers are numerous, between 60-70, and grow in a large circle as different bundles, generally ten in two circles, in the centre of the flower. The anthers are long, twisted and black.

The fruit is typically a capsule, oblong and hard. Dark brown and long, it is conspicuous on the tree right through the summer. When it matures and splits, the silk cotton, in which numerous black seeds are embedded, bursts through. The light floss travels widely in the wind and the seeds are effectively dispersed.

The semal is put to a wide variety of uses — the flower buds and sepals are eaten as a vegetable, and are also food for birds, squirrels and monkeys. The floss, called Indian kapok, is used mainly as stuffing because it is too full of short threads to be spun into regular yarn. It is considered of inferior quality for actual pillow and mattress stuffing. The floss has various uses, from insulating material to sound-proofing and packing. The wood of the semal is also used in the match industry and to make frames, packing cases and pencils. The tree secretes a gum called Mocharus, which is a tonic and demulcent. An edible fatty oil is expressed from the seeds.

Sacred Barna, *Barna*

Crataeva nurvala, Family Capparidaceae

Often grown near Muslim tombs and mosques, the barna is also of religious significance to certain Hindu sects. This deciduous tree grows commonly all over India and Myanmar, reaching a height of 12-15 metres. Most barna trees are crooked with irregular branches, but some grow fairly upright. The branches begin to emerge at a considerable height off the ground. The tree is planted for its lovely flowers, and is often found growing in green areas and gardens. The bark is ash coloured and is marked with shallow, horizontal furrows.

The barna has compound leaves made up of three leaflets arranged in a palm-like fashion on a common stalk. These oval leaflets are about 10-12 cms long and about 2-3 cms wide. The leaves are always clustered at the ends of branchlets and are shed in January-March.

The flowers that appear in the months of April-May are large, initially greenish-white, turning pale yellow or reddish-yellow as they mature. There are four deciduous sepals and claw-like petals, and both are inserted onto a fleshy disc. The large number of stamens are the most prominent part of the flower, and the ovary is raised on a long stalk called the gynophore. The fruit is a rather foul-smelling berry, bright orange when ripe and containing numerous seeds embedded in the yellow pulp.

The bark, roots and flowers all have medicinal value, with astringent, laxative and appetite-enhancing properties. The wood is used for minor items like combs and match-sticks. This is because the wood is not all that durable, although it is evenly grained in texture.

Crataeva nurvala is often grown near Muslim tombs and mosques, and is also of religious significance to certain Hindu sects. It is commonly found in India, Myanmar and the Malay Archipelago

Leaves and the flowers of *Crataeva nurvala*

Beefwood Tree, *Jangli Saru*

Casuarina equisetifolia, Family Casuarinaceae

The male and female flowers of Casuarina equisetifolia are borne on separate trees

Male flowers

It is easy to believe that the beefwood was meant to grow in the Himalayas — its appearance is so similar to the conifers found there. The tree is found in India, Myanmar and the Malay Archipelago. The whole canopy, the way the branches grow out, and the characteristic needle-like leaves that make this flowering tree very much like the gymnosperms that inhabit the higher reaches of the region. Generally classed as a medium-sized tree, it can grow quite tall, easily attaining a height range of 25-30 metres.

The beefwood has slender branches and a slim main trunk covered with a rough, scaly brown bark. The branches grow at a slightly upward tilt.

The foliage of this tree, with its slender needle-like leaves, is its most characteristic feature. These leaves are not really leaves, botanically speaking. The twigs are transformed into green units that can photosynthesise or make their own food. The actual leaves are very small, like little teeth, arranged in spirals around the green stalks.

Male and female flowers are often borne on different trees, so there are male and female beefwoods. The male flowers are organised into many cylinder-shaped spikes. The female flowers are in round heads that often become cone-like.

The fruit is also a cone-like structure, making it even more difficult to differentiate this tree from the common conifers. It is woody and rounded, with seeds that are flat and have wings.

Beefwood grows rapidly, making it a good tree for avenues and garden hedges. The tree has strong, good quality timber used to make oars, house-posts and wheels for carts. The bark has tannins that are useful in the leather industry. The greatest use of beefwood lies in its being a very high quality firewood, considered the best in the world as far as efficiency of burning is concerned — it burns even when green and immature. The tree can fix nitrogen and is highly tolerant of salt and these attributes make it a good choice if land is being reclaimed.

Female flowers or 'cones' of the beefwood tree

The twigs are transformed into green units which can photosynthesise or make their own food

Arjuna's Tree, *Arjun*

Terminalia arjuna, Family Combretaceae

Terminalia arjuna trees

The large and simple
leaves of the arjun are
arranged opposite each
other, they are oblong in
shape and have faint
notches at their tips

The arjun graces the banks of streams and rivers,
particularly in central and south India and Sri
Lanka. It is a large and impressive tree, growing
to a height of 20-25 metres. The main trunk has
buttresses and the primary branchlets droop. The
trunk is covered with a bark that is whitish-grey,
smooth and thick, which peels off in large and
papery layers, in grey and pink patches.

The large and simple leaves of the arjun are
arranged opposite each other; they are oblong in
shape and have faint notches at the tips. The
leaves have a hard, rough texture. The arjun is
an evergreen tree, never fully shedding its leaves.

The arjun flowers in the months of April to
July. Borne in clusters that hang down either
from the ends of branches or from the leaf and
stalk junctions, these fragrant flowers are a pale,
dull yellow and have sepals forming a shallow
hairy cup with five petals. The clusters are
technically called spikes.

The fruit is somewhat oval and has five or
seven hard wings that are thick and narrow. It
is a hard, angular fruit, brown with hues of olive
or rust. There is one seed per fruit. Each fruit is
haphazardly marked with vertical lines.

The arjun is often planted along avenues and
it is a good source of durable timber. Arjun wood
is very useful for construction work where a strong
wood is required; thus beams and joints in buildings are often made of this wood. Characteristically
resistant to fire, the wood is used in fire-proof
buildings. Bridges and furniture are also made from
this wood. The bark is a source of tannin besides
being of medicinal value. A gum that exudes
from the tree is used as an adhesive. Silkworms
that produce tassar silk feed on arjun leaves.

Shorea, *Sal*

Shorea robusta, Family Dipterocarpaceae

The magnificent forests of the Indian heartland are home to the sal, an upright, tall and high-branching tree which creates a crunchy carpet of leaves that is delightful to walk upon. Extensive sal forests also occur in the sub-Himalayan tracts from Uttar Pradesh to Assam as well as in Pakistan.

Sal trees easily grow to heights of 30-40 metres and the first main branches begin only well above the ground. The canopy is round to oval. The thick bark is rough and greyish-brown, marked with prominent furrows.

The sal has a typical form characterised by its branching and foliage. The leaves are broad, smooth and shiny. Each is 8-12 cms long, rounded at the base and with a pointed tip. The leaf-stalk, known as the petiole, is much shorter than the leaf blade. These simple leaves with their wavy margins fall at different times of the year depending on the geographical location of the tree. Most sal trees tend to become leafless between December and February, and the tree begins to sprout new foliage in March. Yet, it is difficult to class the sal as a deciduous tree because of the subtle transition between leaf fall and the appearance of new leaves.

Come March, aromatic bunches of sal flowers crowd the tree. These clusters, botanically called panicles, grow either terminally or from the junctions where the leaves attach themselves to the branch. Pale yellow with small, triangular sepals, the petals are orange inside. Both the petals and sepals have a silky exterior, silver-grey and velvety in appearance.

The fruit of the sal is an ovoid structure with two woody wings. These are the persistent sepals that grow along with the fruit and finally become its appendages that aid its dispersal. The dispersal of the sal fruit is an attractive sight, when they come spiralling down from the trees like little birds. Each fruit has one seed.

Best known for its timber, the sal is classified along with teak, rosewood and deodar wood, and provides the best boles. The termite-resistant wood is put to a multitude of uses, from rafters and bridges to farm equipment and wagon building. The straight trunk of the tree makes it useful as tent poles, pit props and in the construction industry. The tree yields a resin called dammar used in the paint industry and as incense, and also as a cure for dysentery and as a source of an essential oil called chua. Sal seeds are a source of a fatty oil called sal butter used as a cooking medium in rural areas. Sal leaves are used as a substitute for tendu, for rolling out bidis.

The tree canopy of sal trees in the foothills of the Himalayas

(above) The sal fruit has two woody 'wings' that aid it as it spirals off the tree in order to disperse and germinate

(left) The pale yellow, silky sal flowers have petals that are orange inside, with much smaller, silver grey sepals

(facing page) Tall, upright sal trees make up the bulk of the forests in the heart of India

61

Indian Gum Arabic, *Desi Babul*

Acacia nilotica, Family Fabaceae

Acacia nilotica is one of the few species of trees suited to the harsh semi-arid climate of northwest India through Pakistan and Afghanistan

In vast semi-arid areas of the subcontinent, from northwest India through Pakistan and Afghanistan, the desi babul is one of the few trees that can survive — its tiny leaflets fold at night and during excessive heat to conserve moisture; and injury to its branches is healed by a gum which coagulates rapidly to seal the wound.

A scrubby, thorny tree, the desi babul reaches a maximum height of about 15 metres but usually, the tree is closer to 10 metres high, and in tough regimes it is more like an over-grown shrub. The desi babul is easy to spot from a distance mainly because it has a somewhat flattened, spread out crown of leaves and the foliage is such that the canopy looks open and scant, with a lot of light filtering through. The desi babul is often mistaken for the kikar tree, a close cousin, which also has a similar spreading light crown made up of millions of tiny leaflets. The best thing then is to look for small spines where the leaves join the twig, these 'stipular spines' are absent in the kikar.

When the trees are flowering it is obviously much easier to distinguish between the two. The desi babul's flowers are always in rounded heads, with an indefinite number of anthers. The desi babul is an evergreen tree, a most welcome attribute in the hot Indian summer, when it is in full leaf and gives much-needed shade. Very long and narrow fissures run along the ash-coloured bark, in contrast to the kikar whose bark is much more rough in texture and more gnarled. The leaves are characteristic of the legume family, to which the tree belongs. They are compound leaves, composed of many small leaflets. Ten to 20 of these get together to form what are called pinnae and in turn two to six of these join up on both sides of a leaf stalk arranged exactly opposite each other to form the single compound leaf.

The tree has beautiful flowers — a bright canary yellow and very sweet-smelling, with individual florets filling thousands of small round heads. The yellow flowers are borne in the axils of leaves or at the junction where the leaf joins the stalk. The desi babul blooms from July to November, and the pods, about 12 cms long, are a white-grey colour and velvety in texture. The seeds within the fruit are separated from each other by deep sutures which give the desi babul fruit its typical appearance of a string of beads.

The hard wood of this tree is used in a great number of ways — for farm tools, wheel spokes and hookah stems. Perhaps the first local species of Acacia of which the gum was extracted and used, the desi babul now yields a light brown adhesive which is a good substitute for the commercial Gum Arabic. The pods and bark have a 12 to 20 per cent tannin content. Green pods are good fodder. In the culturally rich region of Bundelkhand in central India, the desi babul is worshipped during a local festival when young girls decorate the tree with flowers.

(right) Acacia auriculiformis is a species related to *Acacia nilotica*

(far right) Globose flowers and fruits of *Acacia nilotica*

Another desi babul, the *Acacia Benegal* has sweet smelling flowers.

East Indian Walnut, *Shirish*

Albizia lebbek, Family Fabaceae

The 18th century Florentine nobleman, Filippo del Albizzi, from whom this tree derives its name, must have been renowned for his philanthropy. Because the shirish strongly conveys an impression of generosity, with its imposing size and abundant foliage spread out on its symmetrically-branched, umbrella-like canopy. The shirish has a wide distribution because it is a hardy tree that grows well. It is found all over India, Sri Lanka, Pakistan and Afghanistan. The Indo-China region is also familiar ground for this lovely tree.

The smallest shirish tree at adulthood is at least 14 to 15 metres tall and often reaches a height of 30 metres. Growing commonly along roadsides and in green areas, the shirish is popular because of its welcome shade. However, when the flowers bloom, their heady fragrance and abundant pollen grains adversely affect people who are prone to bronchial allergies or asthma.

The tree's large trunk — often becoming as wide as one metre in girth — is covered in a yellow-grey bark that is neither very rough nor smooth, and has irregular fissures. In many shirish trees the bark, if peeled off, appears reddish from the inside. The real beauty of this tree is in its branching pattern. Arising from one point in the main trunk, a large number of branches spread outward in regular fashion, giving the shirish its broad and open crown.

The leaves, which are compound like all legume trees, are another reason for the characteristic good looks of the shirish. Each compound leaf has two or three pairs of leaflet groups or pinnae. Each pinna is made up of 5-10 pairs of blunt-tipped, oval green leaflets. There is a gland at the base of each compound leaf.

The shirish flowers in the hot summer, during April and the early half of May. The flowers are certainly not striking because of their colour, but they more than make up for that inadequacy by being strongly aromatic and unusual to look at. Feathery in appearance, they are creamy-white or slightly yellowish-green with very distinctive, green stamens. The sepals are bell-shaped and the petals, almost double the size of the sepals, are funnel-shaped. The straw-coloured pods of the shirish can make a lot of noise when dry and ready to disperse their seeds. For this reason the tree is sometimes, rather unkindly, referred to as "woman's tongue". Six to 10 seeds fill the long fruit that can be almost 30 cms in length. One can see these pods hanging on the tree from September onwards.

The shirish is a fairly fast-growing tree and its wood is used for making quality furniture, as well as for construction purposes. Gum from the tree is a common adulterant of the commercial Gum Arabic. The bark yields tannin, which is used in the fishing-net tanning process and for treating infective boils. The shirish is a source of cattle fodder, shade, manure from its dead and fallen leaves, and a rich brown, walnut-like wood.

Large, symmetrically branched shirish trees are found all over the subcontinent, often with pods hanging on them from September to December

The fruit of the shirish tree is a long, straw-coloured pod containing six to 10 seeds

(left) These young shirish leaves are compound, like all legume trees

(below) The shirish tree is popular for several reasons ranging from shade and manure to tannin and cattle fodder

(bottom) Shirish flowers are strongly aromatic and bloom in April or early May

Orchid Tree, *Kachnar*

Bauhinia variegata, Family Fabaceae

The irregular branching and slightly crooked canopy are distinctive features of the orchid tree

The name Bauhinia was given to this tree as the twin-kidney formation of its leaves recalled the 16th century herbalists Johann and Caspar Bauhin, who were twin brothers. A small tree that grows to a maximum height of about 10 or 12 metres, the kachnar is oddly reminiscent of a Japanese screen painted with peach trees in full flower. The tree can be easily identified by its flowers, but even when it is not in bloom, it stands out because of the irregularly-branched and somewhat crooked canopy and the highly characteristic leaves, which are broad, shaped rather like a blunt heart with a neat wedge at the tip that divides the leaf into two.

The kachnar is a deciduous tree, leafless during February through April, which is also when the tree is laden with flowers. The gnarled trunk that seems to show great age even in a relatively young tree is covered with a cracked, rough bark that is coloured a rich, deep brown. Very narrow angles separate the many branches that grow outward and upward from one base; the same angles widen out later, and the canopy has often been described as open and vase-shaped, to the amateur, simply good-looking.

To many nature-lovers, the kachnar foliage is akin to a huge crowd of green butterflies. Rounded and about 8-10 cms across and in length, the rough, dark and slightly dirty green leaves are simple and arranged alternately on twigs. Each leaf has close to 11-15 veins spread-

ing out in fan-like fashion from the base. The apex of each leaf has a deep notch, cutting downward at least one-third of the length of the leaf, thus dividing it into two distinct lobes on either side of the midrib, or central vein.

The orchid tree got its name, *Bauhinia variegata*, as the twin kidney shape of its leaves recalled the 16th century twins, Johann and Caspar Bauhin, who were herbalists

The flowers on the tree of *Bauhinia racemosa*, a related species

When the kachnar flowers in mid-February, there is a sudden and dramatic change in the whole landscape. Its incredible flowers, large and growing out rather abruptly from the main stalk, may be purple-mauve or white with pink streaks, hence the name variegated. Each short spray or raceme has two or three fragrant flowers with five petals that appear curved and shaped like clubs. One petal is always larger than the rest and is prominently patterned with various colours. There are five long stamens ending in big anthers. The sepals fuse into a cylinder. The flowers fall off on ageing and this carpet always surrounds a kachnar in bloom. They develop into pods that are typical of the legume family, long — a single pod can be 50 cms in length — and flat, black in colour with 10-15 seeds.

The kachnar is a good source of fodder. The root decoction is said to be effective against indigestion and is also an obesity-preventive. Ulcers and leprosy sores are treated with kachnar bark extracts. Flower buds, kachnar kali, are pickled and eaten. The flowers themselves are supposed to be efficient laxatives. The leaves are used to make bidis in some regions and the wood is used for making farm equipment.

(below left) The flower of *Bauhinia variegata* could be one of various shades of purple, mauve, white and pink, hence the name 'variegata'

(below) A flower of *Bauhinia purpurea*, a related species

Indian Gooseberry, *Amla*

Emblica officinalis, Family Euphorbiaceae

The bitter-sour amla berry is used in pickles and hair dyes among a variety of other things

The amla tree, which is sacred for many Hindus, is both widely cultivated as well as found wild all over the subcontinent

Best known for its sour and slightly bitter fruit, the amla is deciduous and grows to about 10-12 metres tall. It has a delicate appearance because of the extremely light and feathery foliage. The amla, an important source of Vitamin C, is widely cultivated and also grows wild all over the subcontinent, especially in India and Myanmar.

The tree crown can be round or oblong, slightly spreading with three to four branches arising from the same point on the main trunk. The bark, which is greenish-grey, and silvery-green in mature trees, comes off in flakes.

The leaves look like compound leaves, but are not. Individual leaves are arranged in a near-perfect imitation of a typical compound leaf. The branchlets bear small leaves on either side, in two regular rows, each of which has a small leaf-like membrane attached at its base, where it fixes onto the main branch. These are called stipules. Each leaf is less than one centimetre long and each branchlet measures 12-16 cms.

The amla tree has small male and female flowers that grow together on the same branchlet between March and May. The greenish-yellow, inconspicuous flowers with six sepals and six petals each are borne in clusters on the leafy branches.

The fleshy fruit, a berry that is pale yellow when ripe, is the most important part of the tree. The round berry has six vertical furrows and contains a six-ribbed stone which splits into three parts, each of which has two seeds. The acidic and bitter amla fruit is very popular in India for pickles, preserves and chutneys.

The fruit is a good astringent, coolant, diuretic, laxative and rich in Vitamin C. Fruit extracts are part of hair dyes and shampoos. The fruit, leaves and bark contain tannin. The amla is a sacred tree for many Hindus and amla-puja is common in some parts of India.

Flame of the forest, *Palash*

Butea monosperma, Family Fabaceae

One of the most spectacular summer sights of the subcontinent is the palash, its crown ablaze with brilliant vermilion-red flowers. Unfortunately, the tree puts on its famous "flame of the forest" display for an all too brief duration. Seen commonly through the length and breadth of India, and also in Myanmar, the palash is not a very large tree, growing to a maximum height of 12 to 14 metres. It is deciduous and crooked, with its irregular branches growing haphazardly. Cinderella-like, this unassuming tree undergoes a dramatic change when it begins to flower in the region's dry areas during March-April.

The twisted and gnarled trunk is covered with a rough greyish-brown bark. Young branches are soft. Red latex issues from the trunk when cut. This secretion is said to have astringent properties. The overall effect of the trunk and branches makes the tree look contorted.

The compound leaves of the palash are composed of three rough and large leaflets. When young they are pale green, thick and velvety. The main stalk is conspicuously swollen at the base. The leaves are shed every year in the months of December and January. Older leaves are leathery to the touch.

But the palash is known chiefly for its bright orange, bird-shaped flowers with deep greenish-brown sepals. Since the flowers appear when the trees are leafless, their undiluted impact gives the tree its common English name. The flowers are borne at the ends of stalks and each has a cup-like group of soft, shining sepals. This part of the flower is brown and seems to add immensely to their attractive colouration. The five petals which are the colour of flame are unequal: one large petal called the standard is flanked by two wings and a single "keel" made of two segments,

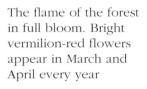

The flame of the forest in full bloom. Bright vermilion-red flowers appear in March and April every year

shaped exactly like a parrot's beak. Hence some call it the parrot tree. Fine hairs cover the petals. This is the architecture of a typical legume flower. Palash flowers are pollinated by parrots, sunbirds, bees and even crows.

The fruit is a pod which hangs down from the tree like a pendulum. With flat brown seeds, one per pod, these are about 10 cms in length. When young the fruit is pale green and softly hairy, almost giving the tree the appearance of being covered in foliage, but it soon becomes yellow-brown and dry with thick edges.

Palash leaves are commonly seen as disposable plates all over India. Fibre from young shoots and roots is used to make rope and cord. Butea gum or Bengal kino is a gum from the tree and is a good astringent and tanning agent. One of the trees that the lac insect — among the few sources of sealing wax — lives in is the palash. A floral infusion is used as yellow dye and as a source of colour for the famous Hindu festival of Holi. To a devout Hindu, the three leaflets of the palash are symbolic of Brahma, Vishnu and Shiva. When a boy becomes a sadhu or ascetic, he is given a palash leaf to eat from and a staff made of palash wood.

The bright orange flowers do not have leaves to hide their brilliance, and are pollinated by squirrels, parrots, bees and other creatures

Indian Laburnum, *Amaltas*

Cassia fistula, Family Fabaceae

In high summer, when the landscape shimmers with heat waves, the amaltas appears in a mantle of gold, as though to distract attention from the scorching sun. Its pendant sprays of canary yellow flowers hang down from the tree like massed chandeliers. Widely grown throughout the subcontinent, the amaltas is common in most parts of India, Pakistan, Myanmar and the outer Himalayas. Although it is native to the region's dry forests, the tree is also very often planted for its beautiful flowers. It is a medium-sized tree with an average height of 15 to 20 metres. It is characterised by irregular branches and an irregular canopy.

The trunk is covered with a green-grey bark that is smooth for the greater part of a tree's life, later becoming brown and rough. It is often very thick in comparison to other trees.

The amaltas is deciduous and its leaves are shed between February and May. These leaves are large and compound, each formed from 4-8 pairs of leaflets arranged opposite each other and are roughly egg-shaped and dark green. These leaflets are about 10-15 cms in length and their appearance distinguishes the amaltas from other cassias, since all the others have typical legume leaves which are feathery. These sprays have a delicate fragrance and each has flowers that have small green sepals and spoon-shaped oval petals, five in number and all five equal in size. There are 10 long stamens arranged in three whorls of 3, 4 and 3 stamens per whorl. The style of the ovary is long and green, growing outward amidst the stamens.

The fruit is a cylindrical pod coloured a dark brown or black. These pods, growing to between 50-60 cms in length, are very hard and are used as impromptu sticks to chase stray dogs or for street games. It is the pod that gives the plant its second Latin name *fistula*, which means pipe. This pipe is filled with a blackish pulp that is embedded with seeds.

The hard and durable amaltas wood is good for the manufacture of farm implements and rough construction work. It is a strong, hard wood, with a great deal of durability. Amaltas wood makes very good fuel material since it burns well. In fact, it is also a source of charcoal. The sweet pulp that fills each pod is eaten by monkeys and birds. Dried pods are used as a laxative. The bark, locally called sumari, is used for tanning. Powdered bark has high medicinal properties, effective against dysentery, skin complaints and jaundice, among other diseases.

The sprays of flowers have round, unopened buds, small green sepals and oval petals

The large, compound leaves of the amaltas

(facing page) The Indian laburnum is laden with flowers when it blooms in the summer

71

Sissoo Tree, *Shisham*

Dalbergia sissoo, Family Fabaceae

(below right) The shisham tree with its irregular branches and crooked main trunk can be spotted growing up to a height of 30 metres in the drier, northern parts of the subcontinent

(below) The shisham has roughly heart shaped compound leaves and small, delicately scented, creamy-white flowers

This is the not-so-glamourous cousin of the famed Indian rosewood tree, and grows best in the drier, northern parts of India and the subcontinent, from the sub-Himalayan stretch through Pakistan and Afghanistan. The shisham is a great, multiple-use tree cultivated widely for its hardiness and variety of functions. In favourable conditions this tree can grow to a height of 30-35 metres, but is more commonly about 20-25 metres tall. The branches are irregular but the somewhat elongated canopy is really a beautiful sight in the harsh northern summer because of its lush and lovely foliage. This deciduous tree is leafless from December through February, when new foliage sprouts, rapidly, soon followed by flowers.

The shisham has a crooked main trunk that is covered with a dark greyish-brown and much-fissured bark, rough to the touch. The patterning of the bark runs length-wise.

The leaves of the shisham are compound and each leaflet is light green and thin initially, turning slightly thick, rough and dark green with age. Three or five leaflets form one leaf, each roughly heart-shaped with a finely drawn-out short tip. They are arranged alternately on the leaf stalk, creating a foliar cloud distinct to the shisham.

In the months of March and April, shisham trees are laden with small, creamy-white and delicately fragrant flowers. These flowers are borne in short clusters loosely branched and grow out from the junctions of the leaf and stem. Each flower, typical of the legume group, has a standard petal that is larger than the rest, two wings and a keel. A single flower is very small, just about 1 cm in length. The anthers and the stigma are never seen from outside, because of the size and construction of the flower. The blossoms fall rapidly and a carpet surrounds the base of the tree during the flowering season.

The fruits are light, papery and brown when mature, flat and strap-shaped, with one to three seeds. They spiral down in the breeze once ready for dispersal and are favourites with birds.

The shisham is a very important afforestation tree because of its ability to withstand dry conditions. It is a good source of fodder and wood. The latter is used for furniture and other items, but is most popular as a raw material for carving. Classed amongst the best fuel woods, shisham is also good for producing charcoal.

Flamboyant Poinciana, *Gulmohur*

Delonix regia, Family Fabaceae

Gulmohur flowers are bright scarlet or orange, with petals that resemble spoons

The gulmohur tree with its umbrella-shaped canopy and lush foliage provides shade to passers-by all over India

(facing page):

In April and May the gulmohur tree bursts into bloom with orange and crimson flowers and pale green new foliage

The large compound leaves of the gulmohur tree are composed of small bright green leaflets

Gulmohur flowers are arranged in large inflorescences at the end of branches

A bare, gaunt tree until April, the gulmohur suddenly bursts into glorious bloom, with vivid splashes of orange and crimson. In May, when the new foliage unfolds, the combination of scarlet blossoms and pale green lace it is at its loveliest. Not as tall as it is spreading, the gulmohur normally grows to about 15-18 metres, but the elegant branching pattern and the generous foliage make the umbrella-shaped canopy quite imposing. The trunk is covered with a thick greyish-brown bark.

The leaves of the gulmohur are large and compound, each composed of smaller units containing leaflets, which is why they are called bipinnate. A single leaf, which may grow up to 50 cms in length, has 10-20 pairs of pinnae and each pinna has 20-30 pairs of small, oblong, bright green leaflets. The tree is deciduous and totally leafless in February and March.

The flowers are arranged in very large inflorescences, called racemes at the ends of branches. Of the five petals, four are bright scarlet or orange and one is larger and variegated. Slightly crinkled

along their margins, the petals resemble spoons. The sepals are green on the outside, scarlet inside. Ten stamens of different lengths are bright red with yellow anthers that have a red patch on top. The overall impact of a gulmohur flower is of vivid colour. The fruit is a long sword-like hard pod, about 60 cms long and close to 5-8 cms wide. Each fruit has many, yellowish-brown oblong seeds.

The main utility of the gulmohar is that of an ornamental avenue tree and a good giver of shade. The wood is used as a source of fuel in rural areas.

Indian Coral Tree, *Mandar*

Erythrina variegata, Family Fabaceae

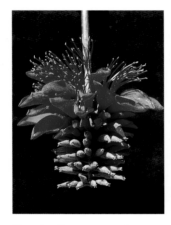

Mandar flowers are borne in clusters called racemes which are attached to the branchlets by long stalks

Mandar flowers are large and scarlet with five uniformly red petals

(facing page):

The Indian coral tree has been important to the people of the subcontinent for years. The flowers are used for decorative purposes and even as a source of a red dye

White erythrina flowers

When the mandar tree is in flower, it becomes a veritable zoo — squirrels, crows, hundreds of other birds, and even monkeys vie with each other for the copious amounts of nectar produced by its bright red flowers. The tree is large, reaching a height of 18-20 metres and is found growing all over India, Myanmar, Sri Lanka and the Malay Archipelago, particularly in coastal regions.

The branches rise from the main upright trunk at a slight angle and then grow expansively outward. They provide the mandar with a very elegant form even when the tree is bare of foliage or flowers. The canopy is elongated and the trunk is covered with a thin, smooth bark that is yellowish, tinged with grey. Amidst the small spines that cover the trunk and branches, fissures in the bark run length-wise.

The leaves of the mandar are composed of three broad leaflets that are smooth and borne on a long stalk. Each leaflet is oval and has a pointed tip. These leaves fall in the months of February and March and the tree remains leafless until May and June.

The most prominent characteristics of mandar flowers are their large size and scarlet colour. The typical five-petal arrangement of a standard, wings and two segments of the keel is found here too. The standard is oblong and pointed, narrow at the base. All the petals are uniformly red. The flowers are borne in clusters called racemes, which are attached to the branchlets by long stalks. The stamens are red and the flowers are not very fragrant. The big fruit are pods, initially green before turning dark black. The fruit is 20-25 cms long and contains about a dozen seeds, between which there are constrictions.

This tree is most significant because of its decorative value. The leaves are consumed as fodder. They are also medicinal in that their extract is a useful laxative and diuretic. The bark is the source of a fibre used to make rope and cord. The wood is used to make rafts, catamarans and canoes. A red dye can be obtained from the flowers. Hindu mythology has it that the tree was special to the gardens of the god Indra. The mandar is considered a good windbreaker, maybe because of the tree's strong architecture. Another reason why farmers like the tree is that its roots can fix nitrogen and enrich the soil.

INDIAN CORAL TREE.
Erythrina indica, Lam.
(¹/₂ nat. size)

Hardwick Tree, *Anjan*

Hardwickia binata, Family Fabaceae

The anjan has very pretty leaves, which when young, are tinged with red. The slightly leathery leaves are compound and each has two ovate leaflets, very closely adhered at their base, giving the impression of actually being one leaf deeply notched in the centre. There are four to five veins running the length of the leaf blade.

The flowers of this tree are borne in loose, open diversely branched clusters called panicles. They are numerous, small and yellow-green. There are no distinct sepals and the flower has five obovate petals, concave and somewhat yellowish inside. There are 10 filaments, alternatively long and short. The stigma is large and somewhat like a shield. These floral sprays are fixed either at the leaf and stem junction or at the tips of branches. The fruit is a thin, strap-shaped pod, 6-8 cms long. Flat and oblong, the slightly rough pod is marked by a series of long veins and generally has a seed near the tip.

The anjan is the source of one of India's hardest and most durable timbers. Crushers, pontoons, oars and ploughs are made from the wood. Anjan leaves also make good fodder.

The anjan tree is found in isolated patches in dry areas of the subcontinent and is the source of one of India's most durable timbers

The bark of the anjan is dark grey and rough, with deep vertical cracks

In dry areas of the subcontinent, the anjan appears in isolated patches, somewhat restricted in its distribution when compared to other trees of the legume family. A medium to large sized tree, it can grow to 15-20 metres, and is slender with slightly drooping branchlets. The trunk grows upright and is covered with a rough, dark-grey bark that is vertically marked with deep cracks. The first main branches, two to four in number, emerge from one point, and then grow upward vertically. The crown is conical or somewhat rounded, tending to flatten out with age.

Leucaena, *Subabul*

Leucaena leucocephala, Family Fabaceae

The prefix su in this tree's common Indian name stands for goodness, in this case utility, and it bears a close resemblance to the desi babul. In fact, the tree is among the most useful of all known tropical legumes. The subabul is medium-sized, reaching a height of 15-20 metres, but its slender form imparts a kind of added loftiness to it. This impression of height is increased by the feathery leaves and light, open crown. The subabul is commonly seen all over the subcontinent.

There are numerous, slender branches growing upward to form an elongated crown. The main trunk is also slender and has a smooth, greyish bark that begins to appear scaly as the tree ages.

The leaves are typically compound and each leaf has four to eight pairs of smaller leafy units called pinnae. These are further arranged with 10-15 pairs of leaflets, small, bright, tender green and somewhat oblong. These feather-like leaves give the tree a willowy appearance.

The subabul flowers in the monsoon months with bunches of small, white "powder puff" flowers that are pretty but not very conspicuous. These creamy-white round heads of florets are fragrant and each has sepals made into a bell-shaped structure. The petals are free and oblong, and there are 10 free stamens. The fruit are long

strap-shaped pods that emerge in big brown bunches, each filled with numerous seeds. These small, polished flat seeds, 15-20 per pod, rattle within the dry mature pods.

The fast-growing subabul has become one of the most vital trees of the region, since it has a multitude of uses. An excellent fuel wood, the subabul is also a source of wood for paper pulp and construction. The plant can fix nitrogen for the soil, and is thus a popular reclamation species. This is also because its leaves are very good green manure. The bark and leaves are rich in tannins. The subabul is used extensively in social forestry programmes.

The subabul with its slender main trunk and light, open crown of foliage is commonly found all over the sub-continent

The fluffy flowers can be seen in the monsoon months and the fruit is a long pod containing 15 to 20 flat seeds

Milletia, *Gonj*

Milletia ovalifolia, Family Fabaceae

Gonj flowers are sprays of pale mauve that hang from the tree in early summer

Looking like an ethereal lilac cloud, the gonj resembles the jacaranda, only in a paler shade of mauve. When not in flower, however, it is a rather plain and undistinguished tree. Medium-sized and deciduous, the gonj grows to a height of 10-14 metres and has a typically conical crown. The tree looks very delicate and feathery because of its slender main trunk and branches and the characteristic foliage. It is not as commonly found as other members of its family, though the tree grows wild in India and Myanmar.

The main trunk is quite straight and is covered with a smooth, light brown bark that peels off in small strips. The four to six main branches grow vertically and begin to diversify quite high off the ground which gives the tree its slender and delicate appearance.

The leaves are typical compound leaves with up to seven ovate and light green leaflets that are narrow at both ends and arranged opposite each other.

The flowers are full sprays of pale mauve, hanging down in a pendulum form in the early summer months of late March and April. These racemes are full of many small flowers that have the usual legume structure of a standard, two wings and the two segments of the keel. These flowers give rise to 5-10 cm long pods with three seeds each. The pods are rough and pale brown and make a gentle explosive sound when they open to free the seeds.

The leaves are a good source of fodder. The real value of this tree is, however, ornamental.

The gonj tree is rather plain until it flowers in late March and April

Horse Bean Tree, *Vilayati Kikar*

Parkinsonia aculeata, Family Fabaceae

Most commonly seen as a hedge plant, the vilayati kikar is a scrubby but nevertheless appealing evergreen. The tree grows well in drier parts of the subcontinent, in northwest India, Pakistan and Afghanistan.

Growing to a maximum height of 10 metres, more often being around 6-8 metres high, this tree has a green and crooked trunk. It is covered with a thin bark marked with many narrow fissures. The real beauty of this tree is due to its elegantly drooping branches and feathery foliage. The green branches are armed with stout and short spines, that have a pair of thorns at their base.

The compound leaves are made up of two to four pairs of leaflet units called pinnae, which is why they are called bipinnate. The leaflets are flat, green and about 18-20 cms long. There are 25-30 pairs of leaflets in each pinna.

The showy, yellow flowers that emerge in April and last till May, are borne in loose clusters, axillary racemes that emerge from the leaf-stalk junction. The five equal-sized sepals are distinct right to the base. The five petals are also of uniform size, a peculiar feature not normally seen in legumes. The petals are veined and have short claws. There are 10 stamens on which the anthers are mounted. The ovary has many ovules and a small stigma.

The long, narrow and straight pod has constrictions between the seeds. Each fruit is about 10-12 cms long and marked longitudinally. There are one to six oblong seeds that are smooth and mottled brown.

The vilayati kikar is a fast-growing tree, easy to plant and maintain, for which reason it is cultivated as a hedge tree. The tender green branches and their leaves are good as fodder. The close-grained wood is hard, brittle and burns well, and is therefore used as firewood in some parts of the region. More importantly, any amount of lopping or pruning does not affect the tree which grows back with amazing rapidity. The seeds are edible and rich in proteins. The bark of this tree is a source of fibre used in the paper pulp industry.

This evergreen tree with its crooked green trunk, drooping spiny branches and feathery foliage can be found in the drier parts of the subcontinent in north-west India, Pakistan and Afghanistan

The flat compound leaves are composed of leaflet units. From the junction between the leaf and stalk are borne the horse bean tree's yellow flowers

The flowers bloom in April and May, and have veined petals with short claws

Manila Tamarind, *Jangli Jalebi*

Pithecelobium dulce, Family Fabaceae

Considering the robust and prolific way in which this tree grows all over the region, it is easy to forget that it was originally brought in from Mexico. It is more like an overgrown, thorny shrub and is usually not very large, though it can grow to heights of about 8-10 metres.

The jangli jalebi is evergreen and the small, tamarind-like leaves remain on the tree's haphazardly-branching twigs all through the year. Sharp thorns grow straight out of the junction of leaf and twig. The slender trunk is covered with a greyish-white bark. Each leaf is compound, with a single pair of leaflets. A single leaflet is pale green and somewhat rough, about 2 inches long and with two unequal sides.

The white flowers are clustered into round heads that grow out from the leaf-twig junction. Actually, it is the fruit that is distinctive, giving the plant its common Hindi name. They are long and curved into helical structures that resemble the Indian sweet called jalebi.

This is a common hedge tree, planted because it grows rapidly. The twisted pods are a good source of fodder, while the edible seeds are a source of a fatty oil. The wood is used for construction purposes and the bark has tannins.

The compound leaves of the jangli jalebi stay on the tree all year round

Pithecellobium dulce was originally brought in from Mexico, but now grows profusely all over the subcontinent

The long, curly fruit give the tree its common Hindi name, since it resembles the coiled Indian sweet, jalebi

Clusters of white jangli jalebi flowers, sprout from the leaf-twig junctions of the trees

Indian Elm, *Karanj*

Pongamia pinnata, Family Fabaceae

For some strange reason, this rather undistinguished tree is widely used for greening avenues in cities and is often planted in gardens and green areas. Otherwise it is a common seashore tree, growing to 10-15 metres on sandy and rocky terrain. It is found in India and Myanmar.

The karanj has an untidy canopy, with slightly drooping branches growing out in all directions. The main branches begin very close to the ground. The trunk is covered with a soft bark that is a whitish-grey colour.

The leaves are compound and with pinnae. Each leaflet is large, dark green and rough. The leaflets soon develop their characteristic brown, dry patches. Each leaf has two or three pairs of leaflets but the top leaflet remains unpaired.

From March to July, the tree is covered with numerous, small light pink or lilac flowers but they are not very striking. These flowers form clusters called racemes that hang downwards from the tree. The sepals are red and the petals are unequal. The hard pod is oblong, thick, and flattened with one oblong seed.

The roots of the karanj are used to extract a poison for catching fish. The wood is used to make rafters, carts, and veneers. Cordage is made from a fibre that is taken out of the bark. Various parts of the tree are used in native medicine, specially to cure skin diseases such as scabies, herpes and leucoderma.

The karanj has compound leaves and small light pink or lilac flowers

The karanj is a common garden tree and is also found along the seashore

Karanj flowers hang down from the tree in clusters

Indian Mesquite, *Kikar*

Prosopis juliflora, Family Fabaceae

The flowers of the kikar
tree hang down in spikes

The desolate Thar desert is enlivened in parts only by the kikar, its bright green leaves and yellow flowers lending colour to an otherwise barren landscape. Commonly found in India, Pakistan and Afghanistan, this scrubby tree can either be quite small or can grow to heights of 15 metres or more. It is surprisingly a very picturesque tree specially because it breaks the desert's dryness. The feathery foliage, the way the gnarled and twisted trunk gives out branches in all directions, the rather flattened top of the spreading canopy all give the tree a strange beauty.

Belonging as it does to the legume family, most of the characteristics of this tree are typical of that group. The branches tend to grow from various points on the trunk, spreading out at a great distance in some large specimens. The overall appearance of the canopy is somewhat oval because of the flattened top.

Kikar leaves are typical of the family. They are compound leaves made up of very tiny green leaflets. Technically speaking, each leaf has 17-20 pairs of leaflets formed into four units called pinnae. Each leaflet is oblong and soft. The foliage provide very welcome, though light, shade against the ruthless desert sun.

The kikar has small flowers that are a pale yellow or creamy-white. These groups of small florets hang down in spikes, which is what the kikar inflorescence is technically called. The fruit is a curved and brittle pod that is about 12-14 cms long. The seeds within the pod are brown, embedded in a sweet pulp. The fruit is supposed to be highly nutritious and is very popular as cattle feed. Humans also eat the pod after the rough parts and seeds have been removed. The leaves are used as fodder.

The kikar gives out a gum considered a good emulsifying agent and which is used in the confectionery industry. The wood from the kikar is used as raw material for furniture and house construction.

The foliage of the famous Khejri tree provides a very welcome, though light, shade from the ruthless desert sun in Rajasthan

A prosopis tree in Matka Peer, New Delhi, with pitchers perched on it

Ashoka, *Ashok*

Saraca indica, Family Fabaceae

The small, evergreen ashoka tree has deep, glossy green foliage

The long, wavy leaflets of the ashoka tree are found in association with the orange or red bunches of flowers

In the great Hindu epic, the Ramayana, Sita is said to have sat under an ashoka tree and waited in great pain for Rama to rescue her. There is also a sect of Buddhists who believe that the Buddha was born under an ashoka tree. The ashoka is a small tree, erect and evergreen, with a very compact, dense and attractive crown. It is seen growing all over the region, in India, Myanmar, Sri Lanka and the Malay Archipelago. Its young branches tend to droop rather prominently and are a reddish-orange hue. The bark is smooth and greyish-brown in colour.

The foliage is deep glossy green, with large compound leaves formed out of four to six pairs of long, wavy leaflets. The leaves remain on the tree all year round.

The ashoka flowers in the months of February to May, during which time the orange or red bunches of blossoms stand out vividly. Young flowers are more yellow than orange. Small tubular flowers appear in large clusters, each technically called a corymb. The tube separates on top into four lobes that appear like petals but are actually part of the sepals, which is why the sepals are called petaloid. Each flower has small appendages called bracteoles that are persistent. The overall appearance of the flower is hairy because it has many stamens that are partly red and partly white. These stamens that carry the anthers are borne on a ring towards the top of the tube that forms the main flower. The ashoka flower has a very delicate fragrance that seems to be more prominent at sunset.

The fruit of the ashoka are straight, stiff pods, flat and long as is characteristic of most legumes. A single pod can be around 12-15 cms in length. Red when unripe, each is leathery and quite broad and opens out to disperse its seed.

Many parts of the ashoka are medicinally valuable — an extract frrom the bark is used as an astringent and to cure haemorrhage; and the flowers contain principles that can be used against diabetes. The seeds are chewed as a substitute for supari or areca nut, and the wood is sometimes put to coarse use such as in ploughs and shafts. The tender fruits make good fodder.

THE ASOKA TREE.
Saraca indica, Linn.
(½ nat. size)

Tamarind, *Imli*

Tamarindus indica, Family Fabaceae

The name tamarind is derived from the Persian Tamar-i-Hind, meaning Indian date. A native of tropical Africa, it is now grown widely in India, Myanmar and Sri Lanka. This large, spreading tree is extremely useful as its fruit is an essential ingredient in Indian cuisine. The often buttressed trunk of the imli is covered with a greyish-black bark that is smooth or sometimes scaly in texture with many fissures both vertical and horizontal. The imli normally grows to a height of 18-25 metres, but looks much bigger because of its impressive, spreading canopy.

The foliage is typically leguminous — the large leaves are compound and each has 10-15 pairs of leaflets. Small and oblong, each leaflet is angled away from the main stalk. They are a tender green and only darken slightly with age. Being an evergreen, the imli is never totally leafless retaining its lush, feathery appearance.

The imli flowers in the months of May and June. The flowers are borne in loose clusters that have 10-15 blossoms each. When unopened the inconspicuous flower appears reddish, but once fully open it is a pale yellowish or near-white colour. Each flower is made up of four sepals and three unequal petals, variously patterned with red and yellow. Anthers are perched on filaments united in the centre of the flower, and there are three filaments that form the staminal tube which is somewhat curved downwards.

The fruit of the imli proper is a flat, long and curved pod, green when immature and a dirty brown when mature. It is thick and filled with a sour dark brown fibrous pulp with shiny brown seeds embedded within. Each fruit is hard and often has wavy margins, with constrictions between seeds. These, found on the tree in February-March, are indehiscent, meaning that they do not split open to disperse their seeds.

The tree is useful in a multitude of ways. Apart from the fruit, the flowers, leaves and young seedlings are edible. The seeds and bark are medicinally valuable as effective carminatives and laxatives. The pulp of the fruit is invaluable as a souring agent in food preparations and is rich in acids and sugars. In some areas, the seeds are eaten after frying. Imli wood is very hard and durable, specially resistant to insect attack and used for furniture and agricultural implements.

The imli tree flowers in May and June, and while the flowers seem reddish when unopened, they are yellowish or almost white when fully open

The tamarind is originally from tropical Africa, but is now found all over the Indian subcontinent. The leaves of the tree are eaten by singers to improve their voices

Queen's Crepe Myrtle, *Jarul*

Lagerstroemia speciosa, Family Lythraceae

The large green leaves of the jarul are prominently veined and turn red just before they fall off

(facing page):

The jarul with its attractive crown thrives all over India, Myanmar and Sri Lanka

The fruit of the jarul is a woody capsule that sits atop the sepals

The mauve-pink flowers of the jarul have thin, crinkled petals that fall off a day after the flower opens

It is quite uncommon for a tree yielding good timber to have such beautiful flowers. The jarul is an exception, and it is for its dual decorative and utility value that the tree is grown. It thrives all over India, Myanmar and Sri Lanka. A medium-sized tree, the jarul reaches a height of 12 to 15 metres and has an attractive, slightly irregular crown. At times the crown is rounded and fairly symmetrical. The jarul can vary amazingly in size depending on where it is growing. In the tropical jungles, it is a large and majestic tree, but in metropolises it can almost look like a shrub. Since leaf fall on this deciduous tree is gradual it is hardly ever totally devoid of foliage. The branches reach out in all directions after emerging at a point almost half-way up the trunk, which is covered with a smooth grey bark patterned with creamy patches. The main trunk is rather knotty and crooked.

The leaves of the jarul are large and it is easy to recognise the tree by its foliage. They grow out from the main stalk in pairs that are nearly opposite each other, and each one is about 15-20 cms long. The single leaf is very prominently veined on the lower side, whereas it is a paler shade of green on the upper side. These leaves turn red just before falling, greatly enhancing the jarul's appearance.

The flowers of the jarul are its most distinctive feature. These mauve-pink flowers are found in large, full clusters at the ends of branchlets. Thses flowers vaguely resemble the wild rose. The six or seven sepals are green and strongly ribbed. The stalked petals are crinkled and very thin, hence the name crepe tree. These fall off a day after the flower opens. The flowers have yellow dotted stamens and a central style.

The fruit is a woody capsule, broad and ovoid which sits within the starry-cup of the sepals that remain well after the flower's life is over. The mature brown-black fruit has five to six segments and winged seeds within.

The jarul is valued for its hard and durable timber, which is widely used for construction purposes. Planks, boats, water-tanks, railway-carriages, pounding implements and oars are all made from jarul wood. The leaves are a good diuretic, while a decoction of the fruit and leaf is believed to be effective against diabetes. The bark provides a rough fibre.

Sandalwood, *Chandan*

Santalum album, Family Loranthaceae

The heartwood of the sandalwood tree is responsible for its characteristic smell which is never apparent near the tree

The round, hard black fruit of the sandalwood tree is a favourite with birds

The famous scent of sandal lies deep in the heartwood of old trees, and it is from this heartwood that sandal oil is extracted by distillation. The smell is never obvious around the tree, or even in crushed leaves or flowers. The chandan tree is a semi-parasite; yet it is among the most precious trees of the region. It is small, thin, straggly and unimpressive in its external appearance. The slender main trunk and drooping branches give it an ordinary, forgettable canopy — the chandan hardly stands out in a crowd. The roots of this small tree attach themselves to those of neighbouring plants and thus manage to survive on other plants' resources. The bark is dark greyish-black and rough, marked with short, vertical fissures.

The small, simple leaves of this evergreen tree are arranged opposite each other. They have a glossy upper surface and each leaf is oval with a slightly pointed tip.

The flowers are small and organised into loose, branched clusters that are called cymes. They are pale yellow when opening and later turn a dark brownish-purple. There are four or five stamens per flower. The bell-shaped flowers are found from February to July. The fruit is technically called a drupe. It is round, hard and black and is relished by birds.

Besides being the source of the celebrated sandal oil of commerce, this tree's wood is one of the best for carving such items as boxes, statues and picture frames. The wood is made into a paste that is a ubiquitous item of Hindu rituals and ceremonies. The paste, oil and wood also have medicinal values. This tree is heavily poached because of its valuable wood.

Magnolia, *Him Champa*

Magnolia grandiflora, Family Magnoliaceae

Variations of the Sanskrit name champaka are heard in many parts of India as well as in other countries of Southeast Asia. Commonly found around temples, the him champa's highly scented flowers are used for worship; they are also much favoured by women as a hair adornment. In fact, this tree is best known for the flowers that give it the name grandiflora. The him champa is an evergreen tree not very common in the region. It grows wild in the Himalayas. It is generally small, but under well-suited climatic conditions it can grow as tall as 15-18 metres. The tree has a pyramidal and dense canopy with a wide crown of leaves growing at least 8 metres across. The trunk is covered with a smooth grey-black bark.

The leaves of the him champa are simple, leathery and ovate, between 8-16 cms long and 5-9 cms wide. While the upper surface is a shiny green, the lower is a rusty brown. This is because the lower surface has a hairy growth that gives it this colour. The leaf stalk is also covered with this hair giving an overall fuzzy look.

The magnolia flower — rather like a rose — has been much-discussed ever since it was first recognised. Very beautiful because of its size and waxy appearance, the flower is large and

creamy-white, and the petals are thick and fleshy. They are fragrant and cup-shaped, shining even in the dark. The flowers give rise to pods containing bright red seeds that can be seen when the pods split open for dispersal.

The bark of the tree is believed to have medicinal properties, and all parts of the plant yield an essential oil. But the real reason why the magnolia is cultivated is because its beautiful flowers and evergreen habit make it a very decorative tree.

The him champa tree grows wild in the Himalayas, and is also cultivated in the region

The highly scented flowers of the him champa are used for worship around the subcontinent

93

Margosa Tree, *Neem*

Azadirachta indica, Family Meliaceae

Large, haphazardly-branched and abundantly endowed with untidy bunches of numerous leaflets — that is how the neem tree appears spontaneously in the mind's eye. Growing everywhere on the subcontinent, right through Pakistan and Afghanistan, the neem's branches seem to have a mind of their own, reaching out in every direction and filling the tree's crown. The neem has a roughly spherical, sometimes oval crown. The main trunk is crooked and although the first branches begin at one point, they start to grow irregularly and this gives the neem its lopsided look. Since the neem is often the first tree to succumb to a bad storm or lashing rain and wind, one wonders if this weakness has anything to do with its architectural asymmetry. Older trees have trunks that show ample knots and burrs in the wood. The bark is a characteristic chocolate brown, broken all along it length into deep fissures.

The foliage of a neem tree, besides being its most useful part, is also a hallmark of the tree. The individual leaves are compound and made up of 7-12 peculiarly-shaped leaflets. With serrated edges, the two margins of the leaflet are unequal in length, one being more curved than the other. There is this underscoring of asymmetry in every aspect of the neem. These leaves crowd the ends of branchlets, giving the foliage a bunched-up appearance.

During the months of March through May, the neem flowers profusely, and is laden with mildly-scented white flowers that look like little stars. These small florets are packed into a bigger unit called the inflorescence, which is a loose, diversely branching structure that attaches at the junction of the leaf and the stalk and is shorter than the leaf. Each flower forms a fleshy fruit that is bright yellow when ripe, has a sweet but non-edible pulp, and contains one seed within. The fruit is called a drupe.

The neem tree is now making waves all over the world as a 'miracle tree' for solving global problems. Azadirachtin, the most important chemical present in the leaves and seeds, is being proven as an efficient biopesticide. Neem is also being tested as a safe contraceptive, a regulator of nitrogen in the soil and for a multitude of purposes in the cosmetics and toiletries industry as well as the agrochemicals industry.

To most Indians, the neem has for centuries been the symbol of good health and harbinger of good times. Indian homesteads have used traditional neem remedies for general protection from pests, as mosquito repellents, and as a broad-spectrum antiseptic. On finishing death rites, Hindus chew and spit neem leaves at the cremation ground; perhaps this practice began to combat any infection that one could contract there. Neem twigs are waved over the heads of newly-weds in many parts of India, and in some places, the bitter young leaves and flowers are consumed on Hindu New Year's Day to ward off illness during the coming year.

The neem tree grows everywhere on the subcontinent, and has been a symbol of good health for centuries

Neem leaves have been used as an anti-infective in India for hundreds of years

The slightly scented white neem flowers look like little stars

Kernels of neem seeds

The neem tree has a characteristic chocolate brown bark with deep fissures

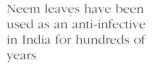

Jackfruit, *Kathal*

Artocarpus heterophyllus, Family Moraceae

The jackfruit tree has a dense crown of shiny green foliage

The jackfruit has the distinction of bearing the largest edible fruit in the world. Roughly oval in shape, their skin covered with innumerable green conical studs, these enormous fruits may weigh as much as 45 kg. The jackfruit has an attractive branching pattern and a very dense crown of glossy green foliage. The rough bark is somewhat warty and dark grey-brown. The crown is almost conical but often becomes round as the tree grows older.

The leaves are thick and shiny on the upper surface, pale, whitish-green, and covered with stiff hairs on the lower. They are simple leaves with broad, almost oval blades and prominent midribs, leathery to the touch. They grow in an alternate manner clustered together at the ends of branches. Younger leaves tend to be slightly lobed in comparison with older ones.

When the flowers are still buds, they are enveloped in large sheaths that fall off later. The upright male and female flowers are distinct, although they grow on the same tree and are characteristically found growing on what are called receptacles. Numerous small male florets cover a stout cylinder that is about 5-10 cms long. When the sheaths fall off, the cylinders, borne on the ends of twigs, appear dense and yellow. Female flowers are found in slightly prickly heads that grow out of the main branches

The roughly oval jackfruit have skin that is covered with conical studs

and trunks directly. The flowering season is normally February and March.

The fruit, found in the summer months, is huge and delicious when ripe except that the taste for the jackfruit is an acquired one — not everyone is able to relish its strong and unusual flavour. It is most commonly eaten in southern India, in unripe form as a vegetable and as a fruit when ripe. It is found hanging on short stalks or sometimes growing right off the main branch of the tree. The ripe fruit is green on the outside, but a bright canary yellow inside. The numerous seeds are smooth, hard and oval, and are also cooked and consumed. They are covered with a thin, membranous and slightly gelatinous coat. Each seed is covered with a yellow pulpy structure which is the edible part of the fruit.

Most of the jackfruit tree's utility emerges from its fruit alone. The ripe fruit is eaten, and it is a very effective laxative. The leaves are good fodder that even elephants relish. Medicinally they are good wound healers. Jackfruit wood is often used for making simple furniture and for the average kind of carpentry work. A yellow dye is extracted from the yellow heartwood and, especially in Myanmar this is used to colour the robes of Buddhist monks.

Banyan Tree, *Bargad*

Ficus bengalensis, Family Moraceae

The banyan tree is everygreen with a canopy of dark green leaves on many spreading branches

The main trunk of a banyan tree is actually an amalgamation of several aerial roots

In the National Botanical Gardens, Calcutta, there is a venerable old banyan tree whose crown measures 377 metres in circumference, and which is supported by more than 1,000 root pillars. There are many other centuries-old banyans in the region — one in Adyar, Madras and another in Sri Lanka. Indeed, its spectacular size is the most striking attribute of the tree.

Although it may not grow to very great heights, reaching a maximum of 20-22 metres, this massive, spreading representative of the fig family is one of the most imposing trees of the landscape. Since the main trunk is actually an amalgamation of many aerial roots, it never appears smoothly cylindrical. It is covered with a thin and smooth, grey bark that peels off in irregular strips. The most distinctive feature of all figs is the vast number of aerial roots that grow firmly downwards, first feeding on moisture from the air, then penetrating the soil.

The bargad is evergreen and its canopy is filled with dark green leaves borne on numerous, spreading branches. The canopy is also broken in its generous spread by many hanging roots. The tree is a haven for a great number of birds and small animals.

The leaves of the bargad are the best feature to distinguish it from other figs that also grow as luxuriantly and as commonly in the region. Dark green with light green veins, they are broadly ovate and leathery. The leaf stalk is thick, with two small stipules, leaf-like structures that cover the leaf buds. The bargad leaves have slightly rounded tips which distinguish it from other trees of the same group.

Few people know that the bargad actually has flowers, because they are never seen in bloom. The fact is that the small male and female flowers are enclosed within a fleshy compartment called the receptacle, or cup, and this totally develops into the fig fruit. The fig also has a wasp within, and each kind of fig has its own associated species of wasp. Both the tree and the insect cannot survive without the other. The wasp pollinates the flowers. The fruit, red when ripe, are attached in pairs at the junction of leaf and branch.

The banyan tree has many uses, not the least being its great shade and ability to protect because of its size. The fruit is eaten in times of drought. The infusion of the bark is believed to be effective against dysentery and diabetes and the latex is beneficial against rheumatism. The wood is suitable for making furniture and implements, but the bargad, like other figs, is considered sacred, records indicate that this was one of the trees of great religious importance during the Vedic period.

The dark green leaves with light green veins are broadly ovate and leathery

Ripe, red fruit are attached in pairs at the junction of leaf and branch

Banyan trees are home to many birds and small animals throughout the subcontinent

Persian Lilac, *Bakain*

Melia azedarach, Family Meliaceae

The Persian lilac grows to about 12–15 metres, with asymmetrically spaced branches

The Persian lilac closely resembles the neem tree. About 12-15 metres tall, its branches grow out in all directions and are quite asymmetrically spaced. The canopy is of moderate size. The trunk is covered with a grey or greyish-brown bark marked with shallow length-wise fissures.

The typical leaves of this deciduous tree that grows in northern India, Pakistan and Afghanistan, are compound and there are 3-12 leaflets in each sub-unit of the leaf, called the pinna. These leaves, a bright, light green, have jagged edges with pointed tips adding to the neem-like appearance.

From March to May, the Persian lilac is covered with thousands of florets that are tiny, lilac with hues of blue and very fragrant. Each floret, with five petals and a purple staminal tube, is clustered along with many others into a loose, branched inflorescence. The golden yellow fruit is technically called a drupe, rounded and filled with a soft pulp.

The wood of this tree is put to a variety of uses, from making toys, packing cases and musical instruments to styling ornamental veneers. The seeds are rich in an oil that is used to make soap. The leaf extract is an effective diuretic and antihelminthic. The bark, fruit and leaves have insect-repellent properties.

The Persian lilac blooms from March to May and is smothered with thousands of frangrant flowers. The florets are tiny, each with five petals and a purple staminal tube

Java Fig, *Pimpri*

Ficus benjamina, Family Moraceae

Wherever the Java fig grows, it becomes, quite naturally, the home of innumerable crows, attracted by the sweetness of their small fruit. Another large tree as all figs are, the Java fig has a characteristic, spreading canopy. The drooping branches distinguish it from other figs but the roots are as strong and all-pervasive. The tree is evergreen. All the main branches are slender and the main trunk is also quite thin. The tree grows to about 12 metres, and has a sagging form. It is found all over India, Myanmer, Sri Lanka and the Malay Archipelago.

The typical aerial roots are prolific, especially when the plant is growing in its natural habitat, and tend to strangulate the tree once they have fully grown. These strangulated figs are common only in the depths of the forests where the tree grows wild, but such prolific root growth is unusual in cultivated specimens.

The thin and rough leaves are somewhat elliptical and suddenly taper into a pointed tip. Simple and with prominent stalks they are leathery to the touch and have the noticeable veins typical of the whole group.

The flowers are borne in the receptacles that are again a typical feature of the whole genus. These are seen on the tree in October, and they are without stalks, found in leaf axils, either paired or alone. The small fruit is dark red when it ripens and just about 2-3 cms in diameter. It is borne directly on the tree and has no stalk of its own.

The elegant Java fig is planted mainly for ornamental purposes and it also provides a lot of shade. The bark is used in rope-making and the wood is used to make match-boxes. The leaves have medicinal importance — a decoction of the leaves is applied along with oil to cure ulcers. Young specimens are popular indoor plants. The tree is often found in and around Hindu temples, considered religiously significant like most of the figs.

Ficus benjamina has a spreading canopy, characteristic of the fig family

The leaves of
Ficus benjamina

The leaves of *Ficus virens*

The leaves of *Ficus elastica*, a species related to *Ficus bengalensis*

Flowers of *Ficus benjamina* on a twig

A barbet eating the fruit of *Ficus glomerata*, a related species

The fruit of *Ficus virens*, a related species

Bodhi Tree, *Peepal*

Ficus religiosa, Family Moraceae

Referred to in Vedic times, the peepal is unrivalled in antiquity and the degree of veneration accorded to it. The famous peepal tree in Sri Lanka is believed to be 2,500 years old. Sacred to Buddhists, it is the tree under which Prince Siddhartha attained nirvana or enlightenment. Hindus associate the tree with the three gods Brahma, Vishnu and Shiva. In fact, Vishnu is said to have been born under a peepal and it is therefore regarded as a manifestation of Vishnu. Generally considered a Brahmin tree, indeed a Brahmin itself, it is often invested with the sacred triple cord. In such reverence is it held that it is forbidden to fell it, harm it or utilise it in any manner.

The peepal tree is always distinct from all other figs because it has very glossy leaves that taper out for at least 3-4 cms at the tip. Reaching 18-25 metres in height, its wide-spreading branches can often be really extensive, growing out in the manner typical of all figs. Another keystone species of the region, the peepal, like the bargad, grows happily out of walls of monuments, and harbours numerous birds, insects and small arboreal animals. The tree is found all over the subcontinent. The smooth, whitish-grey bark covers the gnarled and knotted trunk, with its many holes and burrs. Numerous stout branches grow out from the same point and spread in all directions. Therefore, the peepal canopy is often flattened at the top except that the tree is so large, people often miss noticing the tip.

The leaves of the peepal tree are its most picturesque feature. They are a dark and shiny green, heart-shaped and tapered at the end. About 15-20 cms long and 10-12 cms wide, each leaf is simple, borne on a long stalk, and prominently veined with a lovely pattern. When the leaves are young and coloured a coppery green, the veins are rosy. Later, the leaf becomes a bluish-green and the veins become whitish.

The flowers are not visible, being enclosed within fleshy cup-like structures called receptacles. The male flowers are few and found near the mouth of the cup, and sometimes there are no male flowers at all. The peepal has its own resident wasps that effect pollination and aid the formation of the figs that are borne in pairs at the leaf-stalk junctions.

As the tree is extremely sacred for both Buddhists and Hindus, it is found growing near temples and monasteries. A milky latex oozes from all parts when cut or incised. This latex is hardened and used for filling gaps in damaged ornaments. The leaves are lopped for fodder. When dry, they reveal an intact and beautiful lattice of veins, which is why they are used in a variety of art work as a base for painting and crafts.

The peepal tree is sacred to both Buddhists and Hindhus and is often found near temples and monasteries

Young leaves of *Ficus religiosa* growing from an old stump

The leaves of *Ficus religiosa* are different from other figs since they are very glossy and taper out for at least 3-4 cms at the tip

Worship of the peepal tree is common throughout India

(facing page) Young leaf of *Ficus religiosa*

Banana, *Kela*

Musa x paradisiaca, Family Musaceae

Banana trees are cultivated all across the region, particularly in the south of India

Banana flowers are unique in that they become fruits without fertilisation

The word *Musa* is derived from Antonio Musa, physician to the first Roman emperor, and *paradisiaca* means paradise, where this tree is said to have first flourished. Considerable religious significance is attached to the banana tree in India — in the Western Ghats it is believed to be the goddess Nanda Devi, and in Bengal it is sacred to the goddess Kali. Marriage podiums are built with banana stalks at the four corners, which is considered auspicious.

The banana is actually a large herb — persistent bases of the closely sheathed leaves form the main stalk, therefore it cannot be called a true stem or trunk. It is fleshy and fibrous and much of it remains underground. This particular species of *Musa* is a hybrid, and is called the cultivated banana produced for humans.

Very common in the south of India, where it finds the best conditions suited for its growth, the banana reaches a maximum height of about 8 metres. It is easily recognised by the huge fronds that are the banana leaves. Since there is no true stem, there are no branches. The leaves have a short stalk covered with a sheath and then there is a large, oblong or almost rectangular blade. The tender green leaves have a strong groove for a central vein on which both sides parallel veins run at right angles to the

 108

main vein. These veins go right to the end of the leaf blade on both sides, which is why banana leaves are so easily torn when buffeted by the wind. The spirally arranged leaves form an apical cluster, typical of this tree form.

The most prominent structure of a banana flower cluster is the purple or deep red boat-shaped covering. These are bracts protecting the yellow flowers that grow in spikes. The interesting feature about the banana flower is that it becomes a fruit without the usual process of fertilisation. These small tubular flowers within the large and fleshy bracts become tiny bananas and the bunch develops to give one of the most common fruits of the region.

The banana plant has a multitude of uses. Besides its religious significance, the fruit itself is consumed in a variety of ways — the ripe fruit is eaten; unripe, it is fried or cooked in curries. Banana leaves are the best disposable, totally bio-degradable plates to eat from. The fibre of the banana is good for cordage and baskets. Other parts of the plant, the tender stalks and young inflorescences are all cooked and consumed in a variety of ways. The skin of the fruit is used in dyeing and the sap contains tannin which leaves a black stain that can be used as marking ink.

The banana is one of the most common fruits of the region

The small tubular flowers within the bracts become small bananas

Ripe bananas are either eaten raw or fried and cooked in curries

Black Mulberry, *Shehtut*

Morus nigra, Family Moraceae

The mulberry owes its fame to the fact that its leaves form the principal food for the silkworm, provider of the world's most highly prized yarn. This is especially true of the white mulberry, known as *Morus alba*. A very common sight all over the region, especially in India, Pakistan and Afghanistan. This mulberry is known for the dark, wine-coloured fruit that it bears in the early summer months and for which it is generally cultivated. This member of the peepal tree family is small, sometimes just a large shrub. The 10-12 metre tall tree is deciduous, shedding its leaves in the months of January and February.

The slightly crooked trunk is covered with a smooth, reddish-brown bark with characteristic spots and the branches grow outward quite haphazardly. Mulberry leaves are simple and somewhat hairy, and can vary in shape on the same twig. They are roughly oval and usually have three lobes. Arranged in alternate fashion on the twig, the leaves have toothed margins, a slightly heart-shaped base and a pointed tip.

The green mulberry flowers are inconspicuous and quite ordinary, but they are certainly precious considering the delicious fruit that they give rise to. These green flowers are called catkins; male and female flowers are separate and distinct, often found on different branches. The individual flowers of these bunches are hardly distinct and the male inflorescence differs from the female in that it is less compact.

The female catkin develops into the fleshy, succulent and tasty fruit called shehtut in northern and northwestern India. The purple fruit are so soft that they are often damaged when falling from the tree or even while on the branches. The black mulberry is grown for this fruit which can either be eaten fresh or prepared into jellies and other preserves. Some people make sherbet or a fruity wine from the mulberry. The wood is used for tool handles, sports goods like badminton and tennis rackets, and the branchlets are utilised in basket-making. The bark yields a rough fibre.

Leaves and fruit of *Morus nigra* or the mulberry. These leaves provide food for silkworms

The purple fruit of *Morus nigra* is enjoyed across the region

The *Morus nigra* tree is a common sight across the subcontinent, particularly the northern areas

(facing page):

This small, pretty, evergreen tree is a common occurrence in gardens and along avenues

Callistemon lanceolatus gets its common name, bottle brush, from the appearance of its red, brushy flowers

Bottle Brush

Callistemon lanceolatus, Family Myrtaceae

This is a pretty, petite evergreen tree that is planted in many gardens and along avenues for its charming, willowy appearance and rather striking, warm red brush blossoms. The bottle brush is often referred to as a shrub because of its size and slender form. It grows to a maximum height of 6 to 8 metres.

The tree has a very rough, dark brown bark which is highly fissured. The furrows run vertically all along the stem. Although the bottle brush canopy is like that of a willow, it tends to be either conical or somewhat rounded. The slender, slightly crooked trunk has many branches growing out from various points, adding to the tree's drooping look. The ends of branches are quite thin, almost like those of a small shrub imparting a delicate appearance.

The leaves of the bottle brush bely its relationship with the much taller eucalypts, that also belong to the same family. They are arranged alternately on both sides, linear and rigid, crowding the small branches. Between 6-8 cms in length, these leaves are fragrant when crushed. They give out the distinct aroma of all members of this family — this is because they have oil glands. A well-marked midrib and neighbouring veins can easily be seen.

The red flowers of the bottle brush give the plant its common name. The individual florets are clustered in spikes borne towards the tips of branches and the brush-like look is due to the bright red, long stamens. The petals, greenish and fine in their texture, are longer than the sepals. The fruits of the bottle brush are cup-shaped structures that stay on the tree for a long period and are filled with lots of small seeds. Each flower cluster is topped by a tuft of leaves, adding to its willowy appearance. These flowers are pollinated by sunbirds and bees.

The bottle brush is mainly planted as an ornamental tree and the leaves yield an essential oil.

Eucalyptus, *Safeda*
Eucalyptus hybrid, Family Myrtaceae

The tall *Eucalyptus* hybrid with its characteristic smooth, whitish or pink bark, now grows abundantly across India after it was introduced from Australia

No one who has driven across the Indian countryside can have failed to come across stands of these slim, elegant trees, their delicate leaves whispering in the wind. This is one of the most common species of the many kinds of eucalypts planted in such abundance all over the region. These tall trees can easily grow up to and beyond 25-30 metres in height. Although introduced into India from their native habitat in Australia, these trees have adapted very well to local conditions. The eucalyptus is generally evergreen and although there is leaf fall, new leaves keep emerging, and at no time are the trees totally bare since fresh foliage quickly catches up.

The clean, straight bole of the tree is covered with a characteristic smooth and flaky bark, white-ash in colour. The bark can also be pink or creamy and tends to peel off completely. The branches may be upright or spreading and the eucalyptus canopy is distinctly column-like and open. Under some climatic conditions the tree trunk becomes quite wide, attaining a diameter of more than two metres.

The fragrant eucalyptus leaves are the distinctive feature of this tree. These leaves are stalked, straight and somewhat strap-shaped, and arranged alternately on the main leaf stalk. Each pale green leaf is thick and rough, with a downy white lower surface. The veins of each leaf run along at right angles to the midrib. The leaves give out the strong fragrance that is associated with eucalyptus oil, specially when crushed and smelt. They cover the ground efftively after leaf fall and when you walk through a grove of eucalyptus at such a time, the fragrance is strong and persistant.

Eucalyptus flowers are small and unmistakable. There is a sepal cup enclosing the ovary and the petals form a unique structure called the operculum, a cap for the flower. Each floret is packed into inflorescences. There are numerous flowers and they have many stamens. The fruit is the sepal tube enlarged and contains many tiny seeds although very few of them are fertile.

The eucalyptus is a very useful tree. It yields a volatile oil, eucalypt oil, which has tremendous medicinal values. A fast-growing species, it is ideal for rapid greening of barren lands. But many experts feel that it creates a massive water deficiency because it tends to absorb all the available moisture from the soil. In fact, the whole controversy is still wide open, but the tree is seen all over India. In cooler parts, specially in the hills, the tree can become quite large. Its long, straight trunks make excellent telegraph poles.

The *Eucalyptus* hybrid, one of the most common introduced species, has characteristically fragrant leaves from which eucalyptus oil is obtained

The tiny eucalyptus flowers have the ovary enclosed in a sepal cup, and the petals forming a little cap for the flower

Java Plum, *Jamun*

Syzygium cumini, Family Myrtaceae

One of the most common avenue trees in India that also bears a delicious fruit, the jamun is a dignified tree with its dark leaves and a great canopy that spills a dense shade on the ground. It grows well all over India, Nepal, and Sri Lanka.

An evergreen tree, it reaches heights of 25-30 metres. The jamun has downward-sweeping branches and its overall canopy is like a wide oval crown. The whole trunk is covered with a smooth grey bark, and is dotted with small pits where portions of the bark have peeled off.

The foliage is dark green and glossy. The smooth leaves are somewhat round, with a tapering tip and closely adhered veins. The leaves are arranged opposite each other on the twig and each, when viewed against the light, has a multitude of semi-transparent dots or glands.

The jamun's flowering season is between February and May. Small and coloured an insignificant dirty-white, the flowers herald the coming of the famous purple jamun. They grow in clusters found on side stems below the leaves.

The fruit is the most popular part of this tree, and is seen more often on the ground, rather than on the branches. It is a rounded or oblong fleshy deep purple berry that has one seed per fruit. The fruit is sweet or sharply astringent. It is eaten raw or used to make jellies, jams and preserves. Jamun wood is useful for construction, making agricultural implements and furniture. Fodder for cattle and food for the *tassar* silkworm come from the jamun foliage.

The jamun tree is best loved for the deep purple jamun berry which is used in jams, jellies and preserves in homes across the subcontinent

Himalayan Cedar, *Deodar*

Cedrus deodara, Family Pinaceae

The common Indian name of this tree translates into "tree of the gods", a term that is singularly apt for this tall, stately and majestic tree. This common pine of the Himalayan region seemingly reaches into the clouds, standing at 60-75 metres. It is found in the northwest Himalayas extending up to Afghanistan, and grows between altitudes of 1,500-3,500 metres above sea level. Deodar forests in the hilly regions are often pure stands, but they are also found mixed with other pines. A deodar is distinct from other cedars in that it retains its conical shape to an advanced age, not disintegrating into the typical straggly pine look.

The upright trunk is covered with a bark that is initially smooth, later becoming typically rough, greyish-brown and fissured. The main branches are horizontal which is the basic botanical fact that makes these conifers so beautiful. Of course, the deodar is different from other pines because the branches do not arise in symmetrical circles all around the trunk — they grow out irregularly at various points. The canopy is characteristically shaped like a pyramid. As is typical of conifers, there are two kinds of shoots, long and dwarf shoots. The former grow throughout the life cycle.

The dark green foliage is sometimes tinted blue-green and this gives a silvery-blue hue to a clump of deodar. The individual leaves are like stiff needles, about 3-5 cms long. These smooth needles are arranged alternately on the long shoots, but on the dwarf shoots they are clus-

tered into dense groups. The tree is evergreen.

The male and female cones are borne on separate trees. But this is not always the case and trees with both male and female flowers are not unusual. The female cones, dark brown and 8-12 cms long, are found on the ends of dwarf branches and each one stands upright, measuring 7-12 cms, conical but rounded at the tip. The wood is a prized timber which is not only light but also resistant to insect attack. An oil and resin from the wood is known for its medicinal properties. The leaf-needles also give out an essential oil.

Deodar forests are found in the Himalayan region either in pure stands or mixed with other pines

Scattered amidst the dark green foliage of the deodar are the male and female cones that contain the winged and triangular seeds for the next generation of trees

Himalayan Long-Leaved Pine, *Chir*

Pinus roxburghii, Family Pinaceae

The male cones of the chir pine have thick, somewhat triangular beaks

The symmetrical branches and needle-like leaves of the chir pine are a common sight on the slopes of the Himalayas

One of the most common pine trees that green the Himalayan slopes, the chir is a very important tree because of its many uses. The tree, like most conifers, is very tall, and its symmetrical branches and distinctive canopy of needle-like leaves give it an imposing presence. Walking through a chir forest is an incredible experience, with the typical pine smell all around, the soft crunch of fallen pine needles underfoot and the sound of mountain winds whistling through these majestic trees as they sway to and fro.

This conifer generally grows best in the lower belts of the Himalayan ranges and is often found forming mixed forests with the deodar. The main trunk is upright and straight, even when the tree grows on a steep slope. It is covered with a dark brown characteristic bark with very deep cracks. The fissures seem to

divide the bark into big plates. The main branches grow outwards in neat spirals and are normally almost perfectly horizontal. As is typical of all pines, there are long shoots with scales for leaves and dwarf shoots, which bear the needle-like leaves. To the lay person, simply pine needles.

The leaves of the chir pine are slender, triangular and between 20-30 cms long. The tough and hard needles are typically found in clusters of three. The leaves are each accompanied by a long, greyish-brown and persistent sheath which does not fall off. The cluster of three needles is actually a short shoot, with a triangular brown scale alongside which is the true leaf and is hardly visible.

The same tree has male and female cones, but on different branches. Since the chir pine

also belongs to the family of gymnosperms that have no true flowers or have 'hidden flowers', it is the cones that signify the fertile parts of this tree. The male cones are about 1 cm long and are found either alone on stiff small stalks or in groups of two to five, and have a thick, somewhat triangular beak. The large, woody female cones bear the seeds that are thinly winged and less than 1 cm in length. The cones emerge between February and April.

One of the primary sources of good timber and an important oleoresin, for which the tree is tapped like the rubber tree, the chir pine is valued for many reasons. The wood is not as expensive as other quality timbers of the region and this is why it is widely used in construction and for making furniture, railway sleepers and as raw material for paper pulp. The resin is used to extract turpentine and as a base for the terpene chemicals industry. It also has medicinal value and is used to make varnishes and paints. Young twigs provide pine needle oil used to make soaps and other toiletries. The branches burn well, making them useful as fuel.

Between February and April female cones, like these young ones, appear on chir pine trees

The characteristically fissured brown bark of a chir pine tree

Silk Oak, *Reshmi Ban*

Grevillea robusta, Family Proteaceae

A native of Australia, the silk oak is widely grown in the Indian subcontinent for its decorative and shade-giving value, particularly in tea gardens and coffee estates. This is a large tree that reaches heights of 30-35 metres. It is very attractive because of its fern-like leaves that make it appear much like an oak tree, hence the common name of silk oak. The branches are symmetrical and the canopy is slender and elegant. The main trunk is quite straight, covered with a much-marked and rough bark.

The leaves are compound and look like the foliage of a large fern. A single feathery leaf has 15-20 pairs of lobed leaflets. Each leaf has two or three pinnae or units because of deep divisions between, and each of these is long and thin or lance-shaped. The upper surface of each leaf is green, the lower surface is silvery. There is a brief period when the old leaves have fallen and the new foliage is about to sprout when the tree is leafless, making it a deciduous tree.

The small flowers appear orange from a distance but are actually a medley of green, yellow and orange. They are formed into racemes that are one-sided in the sense that all the flowers are arranged on one side of the inflorescence. They grow out of short, leafless branches. There are no petals, and the four sepals are small and upturned. The term used for the units that make up the flower in such cases is "perianth". There are four stamens that have anthers and the ovary has a long style. The flowers appear in the early summer months of March and April with the fruit hanging on the tree during May through July.

The brown fruit is what is technically called a follicle and has one or two winged seeds. The fruit is oblique, splits open from one side and is rough to the touch.

The silk oak is cultivated mainly for its good quality timber — the wood is tough, quite dense and elastic. It has an attractive grain, because of which it is much in demand for making furniture. The flowers of the silk oak are an important source of honey and the bark yields tannin and gum. It is commonly planted as a windbreak and protective belt.

In March and April, flowers of the silk oak can be seen hanging down from the trees

The compound leaves of the silk oak look like the foliage of a large fern

Silk oaks were introduced from Australia, but are now a common sight in tea gardens and coffee estates around the Indian subcontinent where they are grown for their shade

Indian Jujube, *Ber*

Zizyphus mauritiana, Family Rhamnaceae

The ber tree figures largely in the folklore of north India, particularly the Punjab. It is considered unlucky to plant the ber in the courtyard of the house as it will make the inmates quarrel. So goes the belief. But the tree is revered by the Sikhs and there is an old ber in the Golden Temple at Amritsar. In fact, the tree is often seen growing in prominence, sometimes enshrined, in Sikh and muslim religious places. The ber is a very popular fruit seen in the markets of the region during a very short season. It is common in India and Myanmar.

The fruit has a distinctive flavour, sweet and sour; and the tree has a distinctive appearance — small, seldom reaching a height greater than about 8-10 metres, straggly and thorny. The bark that covers the slender trunk is dark grey or almost black in colour, marked with irregular fissures. The overall canopy is irregular but somewhat rounded.

The leaves are also slightly rounded but notched at the tip. The upper surface of each leaf is green, the lower surface is silky-white or brown. A pair of spines or a solitary spine is found where the leaf joins the stalk.

The flowers are a greenish-yellow and the fruit is a drupe. The centre of each flower has a fleshy disc made up of 10 lobes. Only when the flower is in full bloom are the stamens visible; otherwise they are hidden by the petals. There are two styles.

The fruit has a hard stony centre, but the slightly hard edible part around the stone is greatly appreciated, although it is something of an acquired taste. Pale green initially, the fruit becomes yellow when ripe, fast turning to orange and brown.

This is a tree often seen growing wild in the northern belt of the region. The ber is eaten raw and is also pickled and a cooling sherbet is made from it. The ber has medicinal properties too, considered valuable as a soother for bronchial problems.

One of the trees that the lac insect chooses to live in, the ber is also valued for its wood which is strong and easy to work. Sandals, golf clubs and tent pegs are made from this wood. Tannins from the bark are extracted and the leaves are good food for *tassar* silkworms. Fuel wood and fodder are obtained from this tree. Being a strong tree with light foliage, it is popular as a wind-break species in farmlands.

The ber tree is often seen growing wild in the northern belt of the subcontinent

The ber tree with its greenish yellow flowers figure in the folklore of northern India

The sweet and sour ber fruit is an irresistable snack for people passing by the tree

Cadamba Tree, *Kadamba*

Anthocephalus cadamba, Family Rubiaceae

The fragrant, yellow kadamba flowers yield an essential oil

Commonly mentioned in poems and traditional Hindu literature, the kadamba has strong associations with the romantic Indian god Krishna. He is often depicted in paintings playing his flute under this tree. The kadamba is a lovely tree with a spreading canopy and flowers that are as fragrant as they are beautiful. The bark is dark grey, the outer part peeling off in scales.

The kadamba is a deciduous tree, found growing all over the Indian region except in the arid zones of the west, and its habitat stretches to the outer Himalayan belt, Myanmar and Malaysia. The leaves are slightly rough to the touch, shiny on the upper surface and softly hairy on the lower. The leaves are oval with pointed tips. They have small linear appendages alongside called stipules. Arranged opposite each other, the leaves have veins that are parallel to each other and can be clearly seen.

The yellow flowers are round, with highly fragrant heads. Three to four centimetres in diameter, they are full of smaller florets with oblong sepals and shiny petals, arranged in such a way that they overlap and create a kind of spiral. The flowers appear between December and July. With the ovaries of all these florets having long styles, there is a soft hairy fuzz that adds to the beauty of the kadamba flower.

The fruit is a fleshy receptacle with many capsules that have relatively few seeds and are all closely packed. This makes them look like black spheres. There are no wings in the seed.

The kadamba is useful in a number of ways — the wood is used for packing cases, beams and rafters, and as raw material for carving; the pulp is used in the paper industry; the flowers yield an essential oil besides being edible; and the bark is medicinally valuable.

The spreading canopy and fragrant flowers of the kadamba tree find a place in an assortment of poems and traditional Indian literature

Bael Tree, *Bel*

Aegle marmelos, Family Rutaceae

For devotees of the great god Shiva, no ceremony is complete without bel or shreephal leaves. All Shiva temples have at least one bel tree growing in the vicinity. The devout explain that the three leaflets of the bel leaf are symbolic of creation, destruction and preservation, the three main forces of all life according to Hindu belief.

A member of the lemon family, the bel is a small to medium-sized tree growing to 8-10 metres in height. It grows wild in the sub-Himalayan region and can be found right through to south India and Myanmar. The canopy can be rounded or conical, and it often looks more like a shrub. Sharp, hard spines cover the main branches and the primary trunk of the tree is often undivided. A grey-white, corky bark covers the trunk, persistently patterned with long wrinkles.

The bel tree has shiny, smooth and compound leaves. These leaves are made up of three leaflets each, although in some trees this number can go up to five. These leaflets are all dotted with the semi-transparent glands typical of the Rutaceae family of limes and oranges. A characteristic lemony aroma is exuded from the leaves. The bel is deciduous, generally leafless in April-May and sometimes June.

The flowers of the bel are found in loose, diversely branching clusters that are botanically called panicles. These are full of greenish-white flowers with four oblong petals and small sepals. There are a large number of anthers, and the flowers give off a delicate aroma.

The bel flowers give rise to useful and much valued fruits that are large and rounded. The ripe fruit is covered with a thick, smooth, sweet-smelling skin that is yellow-orange. There are lots of hairy seeds filled with fragrant pulp.

It is the fruit that makes the bel a popular tree, besides religious importance. The unripe fruit is an effective astringent and digestive, a good cure for diarrhoea and dysentery. The sweet pulp filled with a large number of seeds is used in sherbet, a good cooling agent and thirst-quencher. High doses of marmelosin, found in the fruit, are effective as a cardiac depressant. The leaves yield an oil used in the cosmetics industry. The branches yield a useful gum.

Unripe bel fruit can be used as an effective astringent and digestive, while the ripe one can be made into a thirst-quenching sherbet

The bel tree grows wild in the sub-Himalayan regions and its leaves are essential for any worship of the god Shiva

Lemon, *Nimbu*

Citrus limon, Family Rutaceae

The pleasantly aromatic lemon flowers can be seen on the trees all year round

These unripe lemons will turn a bright yellow when ripe

The small, thorny lemon tree is cultivated across the region and grows wild in the higher, cool regions of the outer Himalayas

This small and unassuming tree produces one of India's most popular fruits, the nimbu, widely used as a raw material for pickles, juice-making and to flavour dishes. It is thorny and more like a shrub because of its small size. With an open crown, this tree grows to a height of 3-6 metres. It grows wild in the higher, cool reaches of the outer Himalayas, a sight uncommon to most.

The leaves are simple, leathery in texture and oval, with a tapering end. They are bright green and glossy, with slightly jagged margins. Like all plants of this family, the nimbu also has fragrant leaves. The tree is evergreen.

The flowers are pleasantly aromatic. The petals are thick, four to five in number, white on the inside and streaked with violet towards the outer side. The sepals form a cup. There are 20 stamens and the ovary has numerous cells. The tree flowers all year-round.

The round, bright yellow mature fruit constitutes the most important and beautiful part of this tree. It is glossy and has a pointed small beak at the tip. The sour, green-yellow flesh, organised into numerous vesicles within, also contains the ovoid seeds.

The fruit is a good source of Vitamin C, making it an effective remedy for scurvy. Lemon oil from the rind of the fruit is an important by-product and is used in the cosmetics industry. The tree, being decorative with fragrant flowers and leaves, also having an attractive structure is planted for ornamental reasons.

Indian Willow, *Bilsa*

Salix tetrasperma, Family Salicaceae

The willow is a great favourite of Indian mini-ature painters who often depicted love-sick maidens under its drooping branches. In fact, the tree has always had tragically romantic associations. True to its common name, the weeping willow, the tree appears weepy and sad, mainly because of its foliage. The main trunk is slender and the tree reaches a maximum height of 10-12 metres. The main branches all bend downward, giving the canopy a sagging look. The trunk is covered with a rough bark and has deep vertical fissures. The willow grows well in India, Myanmar and the Malay Archipelago.

The leaves are long and lance-shaped. Being a deciduous tree, the willow sheds its leaves in winter. The simple leaves have small appendages called stipules.

The male and female flowers are borne on different plants, the former being more common in the region. The male flowers, yellow and fragrant, have no petals.

The fruit is a capsule and the seeds are characterised by a bunch of silky hairs at one end, a feature that aids their dispersal.

Willow wood is famous because this is the special wood used for making cricket bats because of its light weight. The lightness of the wood is supplemented by good strength, making it a popular raw material in the sports goods industry. The bark is a source of tannin and the dried leaves are of medicinal value. Young shoots make excellent fodder.

The drooping branches of the weeping willow ensure that this tree is always associated with melancholy. The wood from the willow is also famous as it is used to make cricket bats

An inflorescence of the Indian willow. The male and female flowers are borne on different plants

Butter Tree, *Mahua*

Madhuca indica, Family Sapotaceae

For many tribal groups in Central India, mahua flowers are a major source of food — they are eaten fresh or dried, the outer coat is cooked as a vegetable, the inner core ground into meal; a thick oil is expressed from the kernel, hence the name butter tree; sugar is extracted from its flowers; and they are also used to distil a potent and very popular liquor. The mahua is not a very large tree, growing at the most to 15-18 metres high. The tree is deciduous and has a rounded or conical crown formed by its fairly regular and symmetrical branches that grow profusely. Since the leaves are also large, the canopy is lush and full. Just when the new leaves sprout, they have a vivid red hue, making the tree easily identifiable. The trunk is covered with a dull blackish-brown bark that is patterned with vertical fissures.

The mahua has leathery leaves, 15-20 cms long and about 10 cms broad, and the oval and blunt-edged leaves are all bunched at the ends of branches. These leaves, with strong veins showing more clearly from the lower surface, are on stalks filled with a white latex. Leaf fall is at the same time as the onset of flowering.

As mentioned above, the flowers of the mahua tree are its most vital part. A single mahua flower is thick and creamy-white. They are organised into clusters at the ends of bare branches and the thick and fleshy petals emerge from deep-red or purple sepals that are hairy and leathery. The flowers are in dense groups called fascicles. Close together, the petals form a kind of globule within which are the anthers and the stigma. After blooming at night the flowers fall off by early morning, forming a floral carpet which is efficiently cleaned up by humans, bears, squirrels, monkeys and birds.

The fruit is an egg-shaped berry, green and juicy. Each berry is quite large and contains one to four shiny, brown seeds. The berries have an unusual, yet appealing, musty smell.

Mahua oil from the seed is used in the laundry soap industry and the wood is used to make sports goods, musical instruments and farm implements. Once the oil has been extracted from the seeds, the mahua seed cake is considered a useful form of manure. Some say it has pesticidal properties. But the real importance of Mahua lies in its edible flowers. Comsumption in large amounts can have an intoxicating effect.

(top) The mahua tree is a source of food for many tribal groups in Central India

(above) Young leaves of the mahua tree have a vivid red hue, and their large size adds to the lushness of the mahua tree

(right) Mahua flowers are the most important part of the tree. They are a source of food, sugar and alcohol for tribal people across Central India

Elengi Tree, *Maulshree*

Mimusops elengi, Family Sapotaceae

This lush evergreen tree always appears as a dense, green mass full of shining, dark green leaves. The maulshree has a rounded, umbrella-like crown made up of highly symmetrical branches and a generous foliage. This is not a very tall tree, although it does occasionally attain a height of 12-18 metres. It is the massive spread of the branches and the luxuriant leaf growth that gives the tree an imposing aura. The tree grows well in India, Myanmar and the Malay Archipelago.

The main trunk of the maulshree is covered by a deeply-fissured grey or brownish bark. The branches begin to emerge some distance off the ground, and spread out evenly in all directions. The oblong, dark green leaves are simple and thick with wavy margins.

The flowers of this lovely tree, seen from March to July, are small and somewhat incon-spicuous because of their size, and the tree's thick foliage. Star-like and highly fragrant, they are arranged in small clusters. The sepals are like eight segments put together and the petals are in two series. There are eight stamens. The fleshy fruit are berries that are green initially and then turn orange-red. Each berry has one black seed.

Maulshree wood is used for construction, making farm implements and furniture. The edible fruit is pickled. The dried flowers are made into a mildly intoxicating snuff and the bark and fruits are used to treat dysentery.

The maulshree is a lush evergreen tree that grows well in India, Myanmar and the Malay Archipelago

Unripe maulshree berries are green, but turn orange-red on ripening

Night Jasmine, *Harsingar*

Nyctanthes arbortristis, Family Verbenaceae

The night jasmine is a small, simple tree that might have gone largely unnoticed if it was not for the frangrance of its night-blooming flowers

The harsingar would probably have gone largely unnoticed but for the gorgeous fragrance of its flowers that bloom by evening. This is a small, delicately structured tree with quadrangular branches that grow fairly symmetrically. It is slender and has a light, small canopy. The trunk is crooked and the slightly-wrinkled bark is grey or greenish-white. The tree grows all along the sub-Himalayan tract and peninsular India.

This deciduous tree has simple, dull green foliage. Each leaf is around 3-5 cms long and oval with a pointed tip. Usually, the leaf margins are smooth, but some plants have toothed margins, although the number of teeth is small. The leaves are arranged opposite each other and are rough to the touch.

The harsingar is best known for its characteristic, night-blooming flowers which have a heady fragrance. With their delicate, easily bruised petals and brilliant orange stalks, they fall off soon after they bloom. The sepals form a bell-shaped structure and there are five to eight creamy-white petals. The anthers, with no stalks, are found in the bright orange tube of the petals. The inflorescence is technically called a cyme. The fruit is a capsule that splits into two parts, each of which has one seed. When immature, the fruit is green, becoming black as it ages.

The harsingar is often found around Hindu temples since its flowers are commonly used for puja. The flowers are a source of an essential oil similar to jasmine oil. Nyctanthin is a dye contained in the orange tube of each flower. Tannins from the bark are useful, and the leaves are medicinally valuable.

In keeping with its name, the night jasmine only blooms in the evening, and its flowers fall off soon after

White Teros, *Kanak Champa*

Pterospermum acerifolium, Family Sterculiaceae

This is a large tree that grows to heights of 25-30 metres with an impressive, columnar canopy. Commonly seen growing well in the region, the kanak champa is found in the Himalayas and Myanmar. The main trunk is straight and is covered with a thin smooth grey bark. The branching is such that the tree has a oval and spreading canopy.

This evergreen tree has leaves about 20-30 cms long and roughly 15-20 cms broad, green on the upper surface and rust or grey on the lower. The oval leaf has a jagged margin, and is leathery to the touch.

The flowers that appear between December and February are also large and very fragrant. Either a single flower or a pair is borne at the junction between leaf and stalk. The thick, dull brown sepals curl backwards when the flower opens. The petals are pure white and upright surrounding the white and gold stamens that bear the anthers.

The fruit is a woody capsule with five portions. It is hairy and, when mature, bursts at the seams of its five valves to disperse the many symmetrically arranged seeds that have wings.

The wood of the kanak champa is used to make packing cases and planks, as well as veneers and plywood. Bridges and boats, furniture and toys are also made out of this wood. The flowers have medicinal value and are used in the treatment of leprosy sores, ulcers and tumours.

Teak, *Sagwan*

Tectona grandis, Family Verbenaceae

Teak wood is greatly prized for its many qualities — it is heavy, durable, resistant to white ants, and contains an oil that preserves the timber as well as the nails driven into it. Aptly enough, its name is derived from the Greek word tekton, which means carpenter. Besides being one of India's most important trees, teak is also a very majestic tree because of its height, straight trunk and broad leaves. It grows well in India, Sri Lanka and Myanmar.

The teak is an extremely tall tree that reaches heights of 30-40 metres and grows well especially in Central India. The trunk is straight and the branches begin very high off the ground. The canopy of the teak is neither spreading nor very dense, partly because the branches tend to grow upwards rather than outwards. As a result the canopy is almost columnar or oval. The bark is scaly and ash-grey giving teak its typical, light appearance.

Teak trees are best recognised by their broad and coarse leaves that fall off towards the end of the year. This deciduous tree has simple leaves that are broadly oval with a rough upper surface and the lower side covered with dense, slightly silky hairs. The leaf is about 30 cms long and at least 18-20 cms broad. Most of the time teak foliage appears a dusty green, turning dull brown before leaf fall. Each leaf is paired with another and the next pair is oriented at right angles to the pair above. The leaves are a favourite with certain insects, and hence the foliage often appears torn.

Teak flowers in the months of the monsoon, with the light creamy sprays standing upright like candle stands during July-October imparting a halo-like appearance. Each much-branched, fragrant cluster is a panicle roughly 60-90 cms long. This cluster is filled with tiny, creamy-white flowers, each of which has five or six petals arranged inside a small round unit of sepals.

The fruit is a nut, hard and bony, covered by a spongy layer. There are one to four seeds within a central cavity. The fruit has a feathery appearance because of the thick clothing of hairs on its outer side. These bunches of fruit are as distinctive as the upright flower clusters, making teak an easy tree to spot.

Teak is widely used to make furniture and for construction work where appearance and strength is important. It is in fact the most popular tree for such work. Ship builders find this a good raw material as do makers of musical instruments.

The broad, coarse leaves of the teak tree are accompanied by clusters of tiny creamy-white flowers in the monsoon months

(facing page):

The kanak champa is found in the Himalayas and Myanmar and flowers between December and February

The large, fragrant kanak champa flowers are not only beautiful, but also useful in the treatment of leprosy sores, ulcers and tumours

The teak tree flowers in
the monsoon season, with
light creamy sprays
standing upright on
candle stands

Flowers and leaves of the
teak tree

(facing page) A magnifi-
cent example of a fully
grown teak tree

NON-FLOWERING TREES

The branches of the *Araucaria cunninghamii* are in whorls, spiralling upward and getting shorter towards the top, thus giving it the common name of monkey puzzle tree

MONKEY PUZZLE TREE, ARUKARIA

***Araucaria cunninghamii,* Family Araucariaceae**

The most interesting feature of this tall (35-40 metre) tree is its branching pattern, which is so complex that it has given the tree its common name of monkey puzzle tree. The branches are in whorls and spiral upwards, getting shorter and shorter towards the top. The trunk is straight and tapering and the leaves are flatish, very hard and sharp. Of the rarely-formed cones, the male cones are small and the female ones are quite large, almost like large balls. The wood of this tree is used for furniture, construction work and paper pulp. The tree yields an essential oil.

The *Biota orientalis* is a source of essential oils and the seeds yield a fatty oil

ORIENTAL ARBOR VITAE, *MAYURPANKHI*

***Biota orientalis,* Family Cupressaceae**

With its closely knitted branches and stiff, perfect leaves, the mayurpankhi was a particular favourite with the Mughal style of garden planning. The tree grows to a maximum height of 10-15 metres. The trunk is very slender and the main branches begin very low off the ground, remaining erect right from the start. This gives the whole tree the appearance of a cone-shaped, tightly-packed bush. The leaves are dark green and seem like small needles with scaly covers. The cones are fleshy and ovoid with typical down-curving hooks. They are first green and then become dark reddish-brown. The tree is a source of essential oils and the seeds yield a fatty oil. The wood is used for furniture, construction work and fence poles.

The male cone of the *Cycas revoluta*, one of the oldest living plants today

SAGO PALM, *SAGO*

***Cycas revoluta,* Family Cycadaceae**

One of the oldest living plants in today's world, this is really a very small tree, growing to a maximum height of about 5 metres. The plant is characterised by a highly scarred trunk that is thick and dark brown, and the scars are from the remnants of leaves that fall off, what are technically called persistent leaf bases. The main attraction of this plant as far as appearance is concerned is the beautiful crown of stiff and perfect leaves that are used almost everywhere as part of floral decorations. The leaves are made up of many thin, linear segments with pointed ends and each complete leaf can be about 2 m in length. The male and female reproductive units are separate. While the female cone is feathery, the male is quite hard. The roots are rich in starch and the seeds are edible. This is the main source of sago. But the main utility of this ancient plant is its beauty.

HIMALAYAN SILVER FIR, *ROGHA*

Abies pindrow, Family Pinaceae

The silver fir is one of the most striking and beautiful trees of the western Himalayan landscape. At 75 metres, it almost seems to touch the sky and its dark green foliage is perfectly shaped in an elongated form. This tree is typical of the conifers with its narrow and somewhat cylindrical crown of leafy branches. Its horizontal branches are covered with straight evergreen leaves or needles 8 cms long and with a glossy upper side. The silver fir is distinguishable from other pines by the round scars left on the branch when the leaf falls and by its smooth grey-brown bark. As with all conifers, the silver fir does not have true flowers, but male and female cones, which stand upright on the branches. The numerous male cones are found where the leaves join the branches, and the female cones are cylindrical, dark purple when ripe, and contain prominently winged seeds. The wood from the silver fir is light and is used to make packing cases, floorboards, ceilings and camp furniture.

The silver fir, which is found in the western Himalayas, grows up to a height of about 75 metres

CHILGOZA, *CHILGOZA*

Pinus gerardiana, Family Pinaceae

The seeds are the most important part of this well-known pine that greens the Himalayan landscape. They are like little cylinders pointed at both ends, and the somewhat hard inner edible portion is covered by a brittle brown case. A medium-sized tree, the chilgoza pine has outward-growing, horizontally-oriented branches that give it its typical conical canopy. The upright trunk is covered with a thin, grey, smooth bark that often peels off in big, flaky segments and becomes rough and fissured with age. The chilgoza has two kinds of branches, long and dwarf shoots. The long shoots are always on the tree and have small, scaly brown leaves. The dwarf shoots bear the typically pine needle-like leaves. Found in clusters of three each, the leaves are stiff and about 6-8 cms in length. Chilgoza seeds are commercially valuable and form part of the region's highly lucrative dry-fruit industry.

The chilgoza tree is found in the Himalayas, and its seeds form an important part of the region's dry-fruit industry

While birds love to eat the bright red berry of the English yew, other parts of the tree are used as fish poison

ENGLISH YEW, *THUNO*

Taxus baccata, Family Taxaceae

Taxol, the world-famous drug known for its potency and efficiency in treating cancer, is obtained from this evergreen conifer that grows to a moderate height of about 15-18 metres. The main trunk is covered with a flaky reddish bark, the canopy is irregular and branches begin to grow out very low off the ground. The leaves, linear and dark green, are somewhat sickle-shaped and grow in spirals. The male flowers are found in clusters and the fruit is a bright red berry with a single seed. The wood of the yew is used for cabinet making, veneers, inlay and carving work. The leaves have medicinal value, being good anti-spasm agents. Parts of this tree are used as fish poison and the fleshy aril of the fruit is relished by birds.

PALMS

The most important part of the fast growing supari tree is the seed called a betel nut

BETEL NUT TREE, *SUPARI*
Areca catechu, **Family Arecaceae**

The tall, straight supari tree often reaches a height of 30 metres, and has a crown of long and firm fern-like leaves bunched at the top of the main stem. A fast-growing palm, the supari is characterised by foliage composed of long, thin leaflets organised into compound leaves that resemble large feathery fans. The supari's most vital asset is the commercial betel nut, derived from its huge bunches of bright orange, oval berries. The seed, covered with a layer of husk, is greyish-brown with reddish linear marks running all through when untreated. It is also eaten raw. Curing the seed by boiling it and imparting different flavours for varied tastes are other common ways of consuming supari. The wood and leaves of the betel nut tree are put to a number of constructional uses and as fuel.

Tall palmyra trees add considerably to the coastal views along the eastern part of the subcontinent

PALMYRA PALM, *TAR*
Borassus flabellifer, **Family Arecaceae**

Tall palmyra palm trees are a common sight all along the eastern coastal areas of the subcontinent. These palms have a distinct crown of large fan-shaped leaves and a tall (30 metres) main trunk that is black and swollen above the mid-region, starting to taper as it goes higher. A thick mass of rootlets covers the base of the trunk near the ground. The shiny, green leaves, more than 1.5 metres in diameter, are borne on strong, thick stalks that emerge at the top of the tree in a massive clump. Flower-bearing stalks of the palmyra are used to extract juice which is then fermented to make the famous 'toddy'. Almost every part of the tree is used — the juice produces jaggery; the fruit pulp and seeds are edible, as are the tender shoots and young starchy roots; fibre, brooms and brushes are made from the leaf stalks; and the stem fibres are used to make fish-traps. A most important aspect of the tree is that palmyra leaves were used to write on before the invention of paper.

The tall fishtail palm with its prominently marked trunk is used to make agricultural implements and rafters

FISHTAIL PALM, *MARI*
Caryota urens, **Family Arecaceae**

A very fine ornamental palm, the fishtail is a tall tree with a prominently marked trunk that reaches heights of 20-30 metres. The leaves are composed of triangular leaflets that arise from different parts of the tree. The fishtail palm flowers only once in its lifetime. *Kittul* fibre obtained from the tree is useful in the making of brushes and brooms, and as upholstery stuffing. Sweet toddy and sago are extracted from this tree and its young leaves are edible. The strong, durable wood is used to make agricultural implements and rafters.

FAN PALM, *CHINI PANKHA*

Livistonia chinensis, **Family Arecaceae**

The name of this palm leaves nothing to the imagination — its leaves are like huge fans that encircle the trunk which is about 10 metres high. Before unfolding, the leaves are neatly folded along their ribs which are rather prominent as is characteristic of the palm family. Each leaf can have as many as 30-50 linear and tapering lobes. The fan palm has small male and female flowers, which occur on the same plant. The oval fruit has a thin covering coloured a greyish or bluish green. The ribs are used to make ropes and the leaves, naturally, are used to make fans.

The leaves of the fan palm encircle the trunk like giant fans

DATE PALM, *KHAJUR*

Phoenix dactylifera, **Family Arecaceae**

While the khajur does not grow wild in India, it is cultivated commonly for dates, the sustaining fruit generally associated with countries of the Middle East. A really tall tree that grows as high as 35 to 40 metres, the khajur is characterised by a typical palm-like trunk of swollen mid-region and a base cluttered with rootlets. The characteristic cluster of foliage at the terminal end of the tree is made up of hard, upright leaves that are in turn composed of linear leaflets. The date fruit is a single, oblong berry with one seed and a sweet, pulpy pericarp. These dates are eaten both fresh and dry, besides being used in bakery products and in the making of preserves. Medicinally valuable, the date is a good laxative and is also consumed to overcome respiratory disorders. Oxalic acid is manufactured using date seeds as raw material. The leaves are good thatching material and the wood is used in construction work.

The khajur tree does not grow wild in India, but is cultivated for dates

ROYAL PALM, *RAISANA*

Roystonea regia, **Family Arecaceae**

At the famous Jantar Mantar in New Delhi, there is a vista of royal palms where these towering 30-metre-high trees are seen at their stately best. Forming a crown at the top of the thin trunk, the leaves are pinnate and opposite and there is an equal number of segments on both sides of the rib. The leaflets are arranged in four rows. Small white flowers are clustered in inflorescences called spadices. The small, fleshy one-seeded fruits are dark purple or black. The trunk is used for rough construction work and the seeds and pulp yield a fatty oil.

The trunk of the stately royal palm is used for construction work, while the seeds and pulp yield a fatty oil

FRUIT TREES

Enclosed in the swollen stalk of the *Anacardium occidentale* flower is the cashew nut, one of the prime earners of foreign exchange for India

CASHEW NUT, *KAJU*

***Anacardium occidentale*, Family Anacardiacea**

The dry kidney-shaped cashew nut, among the prime earners of foreign exchange for India, is produced by this small (10-12 metre), modest tree with a spreading crown and simple leaves. These are leathery and oval with prominent veins. The pinkish-white flowers grow in clusters found at the tips of branches. The part of the fruit that is actually the cashew of commerce is enclosed within the swollen stalk of the flower.

The bright orange papaya fruit has many medicinal properties

PAPAYA, *PAPITA*

***Carica papaya*, Family Caricaceae**

The papaya, a fruit with many medicinal qualities, grows on a medium-sized (12-15 metres) distinctive tree with a slender, much-marked green trunk and a palm-like crown of leaves. The flowers are a creamy-yellow. The papaya's inner edible portion is a bright orange when ready to eat and, although soft, it is not pulpy. The fruit is a good tenderizer and is often used while cooking meat.

Within this walnut fruit is the highly convoluted edible seed

WALNUT, *AKHROT*

***Juglans regia*, Family Juglandaceae**

The walnut is most familiar in its form as the tree's mature fruit — light tan, with a hard outer shell, within which are the two seeds that constitute its edible portion. These seeds are highly convoluted within and give the walnut its characteristic shape. The walnut is a large tree (25-30 metres) with a straight trunk and rounded canopy. Its compound leaves are composed of shiny, dark green leaflets that impart a gentle fragrance to the tree. The flowers are catkins — male flowers are green, with five or six perianth lobes; female flowers are roughly four-lobed and are either solitary or found in groups of two or three. Walnut wood is highly prized for making decorative furniture, quality cabinets, and musical instruments.

GUAVA, *AMROOD*

Psidium guajava, **Family Myrtaceae**

The ripe guava is pale yellow-green with many small seeds embedded in the edible, white flesh. It is borne on a relatively large (12 metre) tree, with a slender trunk covered with a pale, smooth bark, and branches that are very low off the ground. The rough, fragrant leaves are oblong with conspicuous veins. The flowers are fragrant and white with oval petals. The guava is a berry, at one end of which the sepals persist in the fruit, giving it the appearance of having a small crown.

The guava fruit is a berry with a small crown of sepals

POMEGRANATE, *ANAR*

Punica granatum, **Family Punicaceae**

The pomegranate is unique in that the seeds — normally discarded — constitute its edible part. Thousands of these seeds covered with a glistening white-red pulp, juicy and very sweet, are contained within the fruit's soft shell, green initially but yellow-red when ripe. The tree has irregularly spreading branches, a slender trunk and bright green oval leaves with pointed tips. The tree's scarlet flowers are tubular and like big bells.

The pomegranate is unique in that its seeds, rather than other parts of the plant, are edible

APPLE, *SEB*

Malus pumila, **Family Rosaceae**

There are a great number of varieties of the apple, the most common being Red Delicious and Golden Delicious. These are horticultural hybrids that have emerged from the original wild apple. Apple trees are generally small (8-10 metres) and have wide, rounded crowns. The leaves are oval and the fragrant flowers are of varied colours ranging from white and pink to purple.

Apples grow on small trees with wide, rounded crowns

PLUM, *AALOO BUKHARA*

Prunus domestica, **Family Rosaceae**

Soft, pulpy and a deep purple, plums do not enjoy the same popularity as oranges, mangoes and other fruit. The upright tree reaches a height of 6-8 metres. The jagged leaves are somewhat oval, dark green on the upper surface, slightly pale and hairy below. Clusters of white flowers give rise to the globular fruits with thin, smooth skins.

Clusters of white flowers
give way to soft, pulpy
fruit with smooth skins

PEACH, *AADOO*

Prunus persica, **Family Rosaceae**

The first image of a peach tree that comes to mind is of its exquisite blossoms rather than its commercially important fruit. Rarely exceeding 8 metres in height, the peach in flower is one of the most delicately beautiful trees in the world. The leaves are lance-shaped and with finely jagged margins. The flowers are formed into long stalks of pale or bright pink blooms that finally give rise to the plump peach with its characteristic hairy skin. This fruit is a drupe and has an elaborately patterned dark brown stone at the centre of its edible, soft pulp. The mature fruit is usually yellow and pink, with shades of a brighter red sometimes. The peach blossom is a favourite motif on Oriental screen paintings, specially those of the Far East.

Not only do peach trees
bear commercially
important fruit, but they
also have some of the
most beautiful pink
flowers in the world

MANDARIN ORANGE, *SANTRA*

Citrus reticulata, **Family Rutaceae**

The orange has a soft, loose skin that covers the delicious fruit within. It is actually a juicy berry divided into segments, each of which contains seeds. The orange is widely cultivated, especially in Central India, and is greatly enjoyed during the season. It grows on a small (8-10 metres) tree with a dense canopy full of the typically fragrant leaves of the plant. These are glossy and bright green, dotted all over with glands that impart their characteristic aroma.

LITCHI, *LITCHI*

Litchi chinensis, **Family Sapindaceae**

Only appearing in the market for a short while, the delicious litchi fruit is borne on a small (6-9 metre) tree with drooping branches covered with compound leaves that have two to four pairs of pointed leaflets. The small whitish flowers are rather insignificant and are found in clusters at the tips of branches. The fruit is pink to maroon on the outside, with a prickly jacket. Inside is the sweet, translucent white pulp covering a hard brown seed.

The orange tree is widely cultivated all over India and its glossy green leaves are dotted with glands that impart a characteristic aroma

Small, white litchi flowers are found in clusters at the tips of the branches

139

BAMBOOS

The golden bamboo is a grass that is cultivated and widely used to make scaffolding, toys, roofs and furniture

The solid bamboo is a different tree grass in that it has solid culms, unlike any other member of its family

GOLDEN BAMBOO, *SUNEHARA BANS*

Bambusa vulgaris, Family Poaceae

Bamboos are actually grasses that grow to heights of 20 to 30 metres. Hard and woody, they are commonly seen in great clumps all over the subcontinent. The golden bamboo is not as dense or spiny as other bamboos, but is characteristically tufted. A typical feature of any bamboo is the distinct three parts of the plant — a culm, the main stem that bears the leafy portion and stays above the ground; a portion of the stem that is under-ground, called the rhizome; and the roots.

This particular bamboo is rather striking because of its glossy, shining culms initially green and then, as they age, becoming a golden yellow. Some golden bamboos show a striped green and yellow culm that is also very attractive. Bamboo culms are divided into nodes and internodes. The internodes are at least 20 to 25 cms long and the nodes that demarcate them are the junctions where the protective sheaths covering the culm emerge. As the bamboo reaches maturity, the plant tissue that makes up the culm hardens and the internodes become hollow. Branches with leaves are then restricted to the upper part of the culm. The leaves of the golden bamboo are rough, long and narrow, absolutely flat and with multiple veins running through.

Bamboos are well known for their characteristic flowering pattern, called monocarpic, meaning that they flower only once and then die. A bamboo lives for many years before it attains ripeness to flower. A grassy spikelet, the flower has a long style and plume-like stigma that typifies such inflorescences.

This particular bamboo is often grown for ornamental reasons because of its bright, gleaming culms. In regions where it grows abundantly, locals use it for scaffolding and making roofs, toys and furniture.

SOLID BAMBOO, *BANS*

Dendrocalamus strictus, Family Poaceae

A different tree grass, this bamboo has solid culms, unlike any other member of its family. A medium-sized, deciduous bamboo, the bans is closely packed into dense clumps that are a blotched greyish-green. The lower part of the culm has short, stiff branches devoid of foliage. The upper portion of the clump has leafy and relatively slender branches.

The typical joints or nodes divide the culm into 20-30 cms long internodes. When the bamboo grows in dry climatic regimes, these internodes become almost solid, but if found growing in moist areas, they are hollow although with very thick walls. The characteristic sheaths that cover the culm are shorter than each internode, so that the top of the culm shows from the tip of the sheath.

The leaves are narrow and linear, and densely hairy on both sides. The flowers of the solid bamboo are hairy spikelets, as with the whole family. The dense rounded heads of flowers are numerous although a large majority are what are called 'empty' glumes. This means that the fertile flowers are very few, just on average two or three. The flowers give rise to a one-celled, one-seeded dry fruit characteristic of all grasses, called a caryopsis. The solid bamboo is monocarpic like all other bamboos — it dies after flowering once. There are some that flower more than once but the time gap between two spurts of flowering is very great.

Rafters and scaffolding, mats and furniture, water pipes and musical instruments are all made from the sturdy mature culms of the bans. The pulp is used in the manufacture of paper and rayon.

GLOSSARY

abscission the process of leaf, fruit or flower falling from a plant, effected by the formation of a special tissue in the abscission zone.

anther part of male reproductive unit that is generally shaped like a sac and contains the pollen grains or that can be called the sperm of plants.

apical at the tip of a branch, stem or flower stalk.

axil the angle between a stalk or twig and the main stem from which it grows out.

bark external covering of woody stem or trunk, distinct and separable from the wood itself.

berry term used to describe a fleshy fruit that has one or more seeds and does not split open to release these seeds.

bipinnate a compound leaf with its midrib branched into different parts that bear the leaflets.

bract a small appendage to a flower that is actually a modified leaf. It can be of various shapes and colours.

bud an unopened leaf or flower.

calyx the outer, protective covering of a flower bud that forms the lower cup of the opened flower, made of sepals. Generally green in colour.

capsule term used to describe a dry fruit that splits open to release its seeds. There is generally more than one compartment in the fruit.

caryopsis term used for one-celled, one-seeded indehiscent fruit that is dry, typical fruit of all grasses.

compound formed of more than one part, like a leaf formed of many leaflets.

corolla generally the most attractive part of a flower, made of petals that can be variously coloured. It protects the internal organs and attracts insects that can fertilise the flower. The portion that advertises a flower.

corymb a type of inflorescence that has the lengths of individual flower stalks so adjusted that the top is flat. The outer flowers in the flat cluster open first.

culm hollow or pithy stem that is cylindrical.

cultivar a type of plant obtained by cross-breeding and cultivation.

cyme a type of inflorescence that is branched and shaped like an inverted cone, with all the branches and main axis also ending in a flower. The inner flowers are the first to open.

deciduous a temporary organ with a temporary function. Most commonly used to describe plants that lose their leaves during a particular season, most often winter.

deflexed turning outward and downward.

dehiscent generally used to describe fruits that naturally split open to release the seeds within.

digitate when the units of an organ emerge from one common point and then grow apart, like the fingers of a hand.

dioecious when the male and female flowers are borne by separate plants.

dispersal to send off in various directions, spread widely. Generally used to explain movement of seeds away from parent tree.

drupe term used to describe a fruit that is fleshy and has the seed contained in a woody stone. The fruit does not split to release its seeds, i.e. it is indehiscent.

endosperm nutritive part of the female tissue, part of the embryo sac.

fascicle close cluster of flowers or leaves.

frond term used to describe leaves of ferns and palms.

fruit structure developed from ovary of flower after fertilisation, enclosing the mature seed or seeds.

gymnosperm plant with exposed seeds not enclosed within an ovary.

gynoecium the female part of the reproductive unit of a flower. It consists of the style, stigma and ovary.

gynophore stalk on which the ovary is found mounted in many flowers.

heartwood the dead wood in the centre of a tree trunk that does not have any sap.

indehiscent a term used to describe fruits that do not open spontaneously to release the seeds within.

inflorescence a unit that contains the flowers of a plant. It has a defined arrangement of flowers.

internode the space between two nodes or markings on a stem or branch, specially prominent in bamboos.

lamina the blade or flat portion of a leaf.

latex milky secretion from cut organs of plants.

leaf outgrowth of a stem or branch, generally consisting of a stalk and leaf blade. Usually the main food-making organ for the plant.

mesocarp the middle part of the fruit layers that surround the seed, often the edible, fleshy portion.

midrib the central axis of a compound leaf or inflorescence.

monocarpic a plant that flowers and fruits only once in its lifetime.

monoecious when the male and female flowers are borne on the same plant.

node the place from which leaves arise on a stem, generally clearly marked.

obovate referring to shape, like an inverted egg.

operculum a rounded cover or lid, particularly of eucalyptus flowers.

panicle a loose, much-branched inflorescence.

pedicel the stalk that bears flowers and attaches them to the main stem or branch.

perianth when the sepals and petals are indistinguishable, and form a common unit.

petals the part of the flower that forms the corolla, usually the most attractive part of the flower.

petiole the stalk that attaches the leaf to its stem or branch.

photosynthesis the process by which plants manufacture their food using energy from the sun, carbon dioxide from the atmosphere and a plant pigment meant for this purpose, chlorophyll.

pistil female reproductive unit of the flower.

pod term used to describe a type of fruit that is also called a legume. It is dry, generally contains a large number of seeds and dehisces naturally to release the seeds.

pollen grains within the anthers that form the male reproductive unit and produce the male gametes.

pollination the process of pollen reaching the stigma, the beginning of fertilisation.

receptacle the modified, swollen portion of the stalk that bears a flower or cluster of flowers.

rhizome an underground stem, producing both roots below and shoots above.

root organ of plant body that grows down usually, anchors the plant and provides nourishment by absorbing nutrients and moisture from the soil.

seed the mature, fertilised ovule of a flowering plant.

sessile when a fruit, flower or leaf is attached to the stem or branch directly, without any stalk.

stamen the male reproductive unit, that has filaments to which the anthers are attached.

stem the ascending portion of the plant, usually above ground, the main framework of a plant.

stigma part of the female reproductive unit, at the tip of the pistil, the portion that receives pollen.

stipule a small, leafy appendage at the base of a leaf stalk.

style slender stalk between ovary and stigma in female reproductive unit.

umbel an inflorescence in which all the stalks of flowers arise from the same point and branch outward, creating an umbrella-like appearance of the cluster.

wood the hard substance comprising most of the stem or trunk under the bark. Includes dead heartwood.

FURTHER READING

Anon. 1980.
Firewood Crops: Shrub and Tree Species for Energy Production. National Academy of Sciences, Washington DC.

Anon. 1986.
The Useful Plants of India. Publications and Information Directorate, New Delhi.

Boom, B. K. and Kleijn, H. 1966.
The Glory of the Tree. George G. Harper and Co. Ltd., London.

Brandis, Dietrich. 1906.
Indian Trees. Archibald Constable and Co. Ltd., London.

Cowen, D. V. 1950.
Flowering Trees and Shrubs in India. Thacker and Co., Bombay.

Gamble, J. S. 1881.
A Manual of Indian Timbers. Bishen Singh Mahendra Pal Singh, Dehra Dun.

Gandhi, Maneka & Singh, Yasmin. 1989. *Brahma's Hair*. Rupa and Co., New Delhi.

Lanzara, Paola and Pizzetti, Mariella. 1977. *Simon and Schuster's Guide to Trees*. Simon and Schuster Incorporated, New York.

Maheshwari, J. K. 1963.
The Flora of Delhi. Council of Scientific and Industrial Research, New Delhi.

Nayar, M. P. 1985.
Meaning of Indian Flowering Plant Names. Botanical Survey of India, Calcutta.

Nicholson, B. E. and Clapham, A. R. 1975.
The Oxford Book of Trees. Oxford University Press, Great Britain.

Randhawa, M. S. 1965. *Flowering Trees*. National Book Trust, New Delhi.

Rao, A. N. and Chin, W. Y. 1989. *Singapore Trees*. Singapore Institute of Biology, Singapore.

Santapau, H. 1966. *Common Trees*. National Book Trust, New Delhi.

Sinha, Binod Chandra. Undated. *Tree Worship in Ancient India*. Books Today, New Delhi.

Venkatesh, C. S. 1976. *Our Tree Neighbours*. National Council for Educational Research and Training, New Delhi.